JOHN ALLISON + MAX SARIN

THE QUOTABLE
GIANT
DAYS ™

D0596270

Published by
BOOM! BOX ™

Ross Richie CEO & Founder
Joy Huffman CFO
Matt Gagnon Editor-in-Chief
Filip Sablik President, Publishing & Marketing
Stephen Christy President, Development
Lance Kreiter Vice President, Licensing & Merchandising
Arune Singh Vice President, Marketing
Bryce Carlson Vice President, Editorial & Creative Strategy
Kate Henning Director, Operations
Spencer Simpson Director, Sales
Scott Newman Manager, Production Design
Elyse Strandberg Manager, Finance
Sierra Hahn Executive Editor
Jeanine Schaefer Executive Editor
Dafna Pleban Senior Editor
Shannon Watters Senior Editor
Eric Harburn Senior Editor
Matthew Levine Editor
Sophie Philips-Roberts Associate Editor
Amanda LaFranco Associate Editor
Jonathan Manning Associate Editor
Gavin Gronenthal Assistant Editor

Gwen Waller Assistant Editor
Allyson Gronowitz Assistant Editor
Ramiro Portnoy Assistant Editor
Shelby Netschke Editorial Assistant
Michelle Ankley Design Coordinator
Marie Krupina Production Designer
Grace Park Production Designer
Chelsea Roberts Production Designer
Samantha Knapp Production Design Assistant
José Meza Live Events Lead
Stephanie Hocutt Digital Marketing Lead
Esther Kim Marketing Coordinator
Cat O'Grady Digital Marketing Coordinator
Breanna Sarpy Live Events Coordinator
Amanda Lawson Marketing Assistant
Holly Aitchison Digital Sales Coordinator
Morgan Perry Retail Sales Coordinator
Megan Christopher Operations Coordinator
Rodrigo Hernandez Operations Coordinator
Zipporah Smith Operations Assistant
Jason Lee Senior Accountant
Sabrina Lesin Accounting Assistant

BOOM! BOX™

THE QUOTABLE GIANT DAYS, July 2020. Published by BOOM! Box, a division of Boom
Entertainment, Inc. Giant Days is ™ & © 2020 John Allison. All rights reserved.
BOOM! Box™ and the BOOM! Box logo are trademarks of Boom Entertainment,
Inc., registered in various countries and categories. All characters, events, and
institutions depicted herein are fictional. Any similarity between any of the
names, characters, persons, events, and/or institutions in this publication is
actual names, characters, and persons, whether living or dead, events, and/
or institutions is unintended and purely coincidental. BOOM! Box does not read or
accept unsolicited submissions of ideas, stories, or artwork.

BOOM! Studios, 5670 Wilshire Boulevard, Suite 400, Los Angeles, CA 90036-5679.
Printed in China. First Printing.

ISBN: 978-1-68415-569-9 eISBN: 978-1-64144-735-5

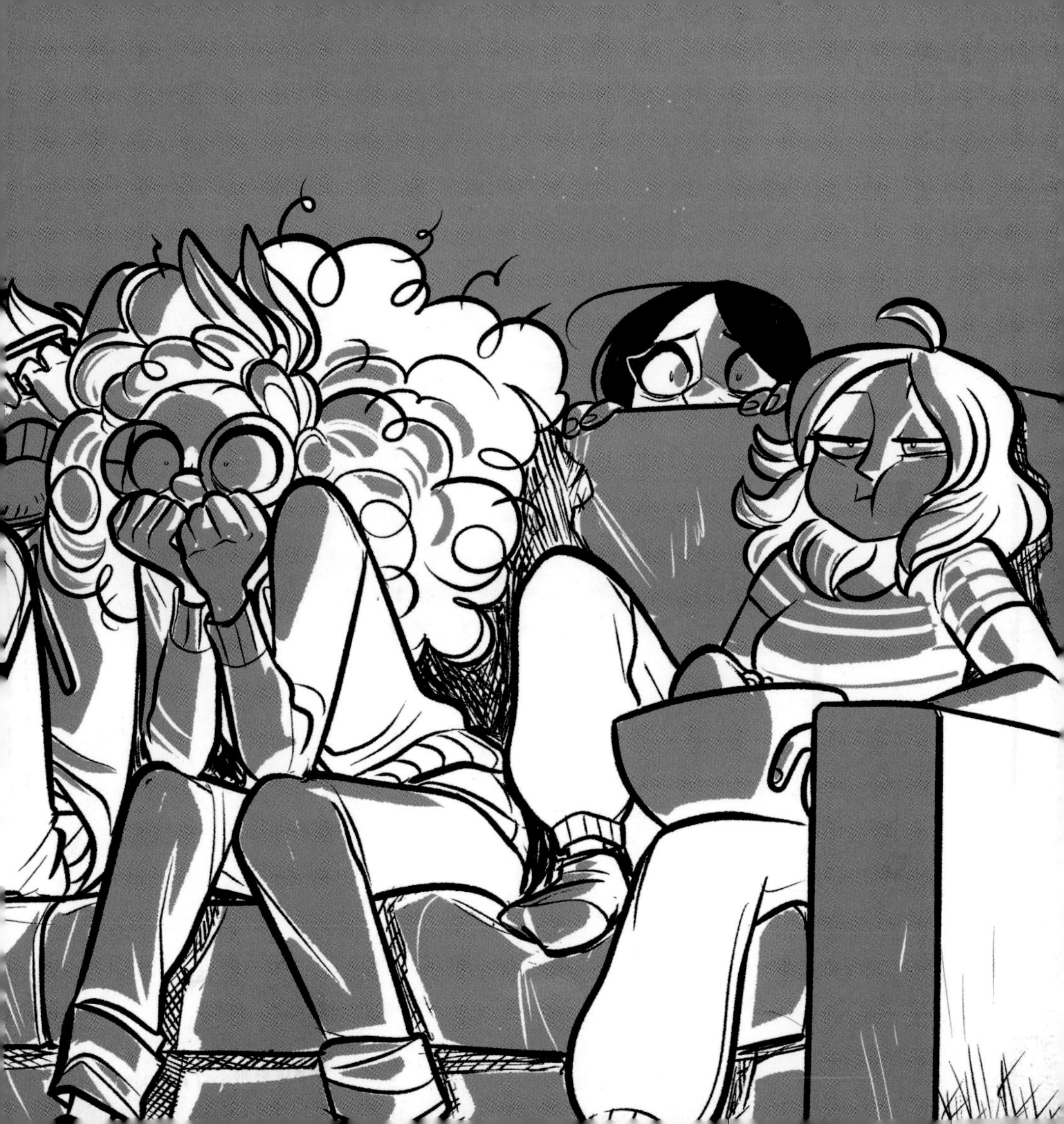

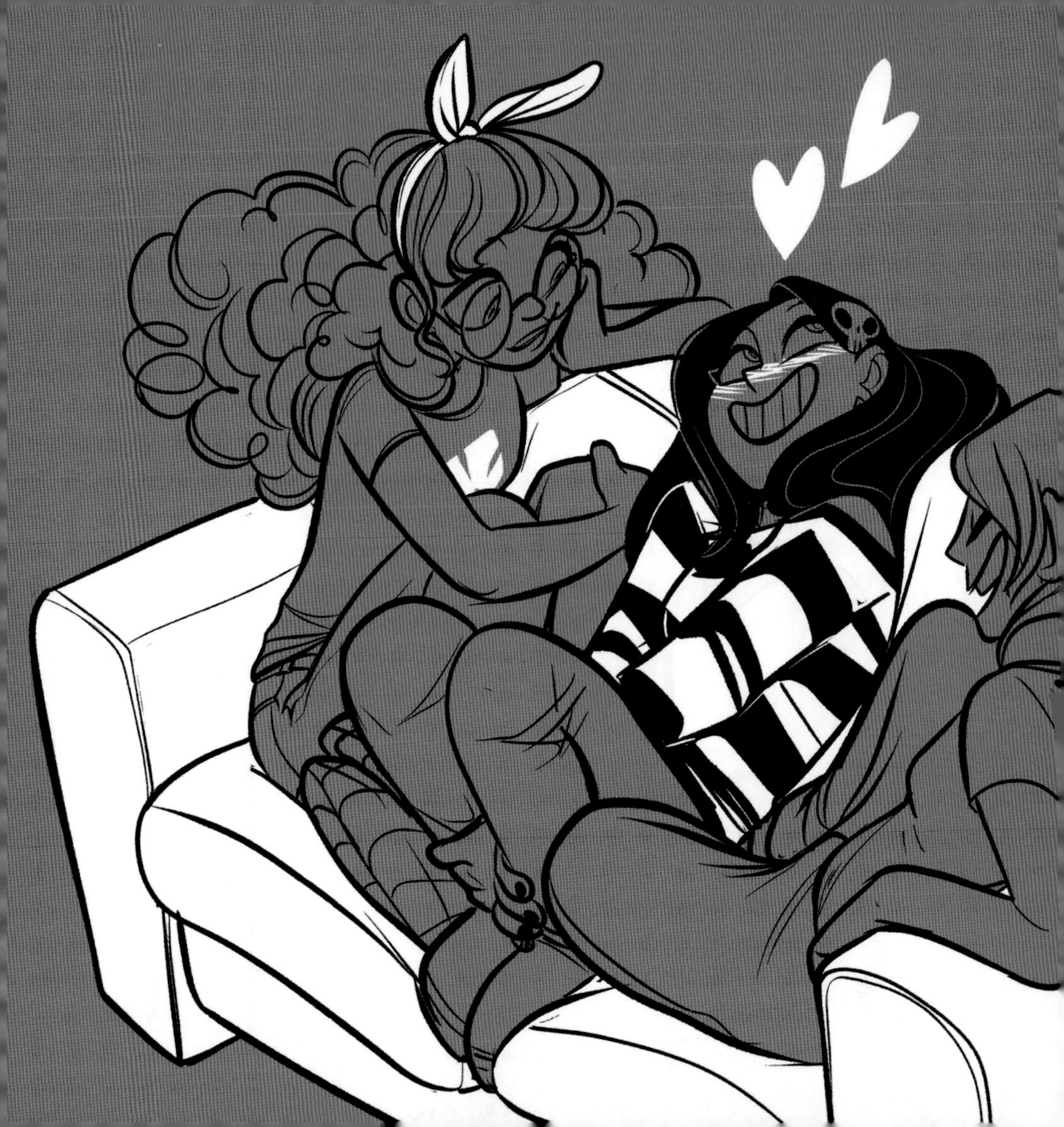

Created & Written by
JOHN ALLISON

Illustrated by
MAX SARIN & LISSA TREIMAN

Cover by
MAX SARIN

Designers
SCOTT NEWMAN & CHELSEA ROBERTS

Associate Editor
SOPHIE PHILIPS-ROBERTS

Editor
SHANNON WATTERS

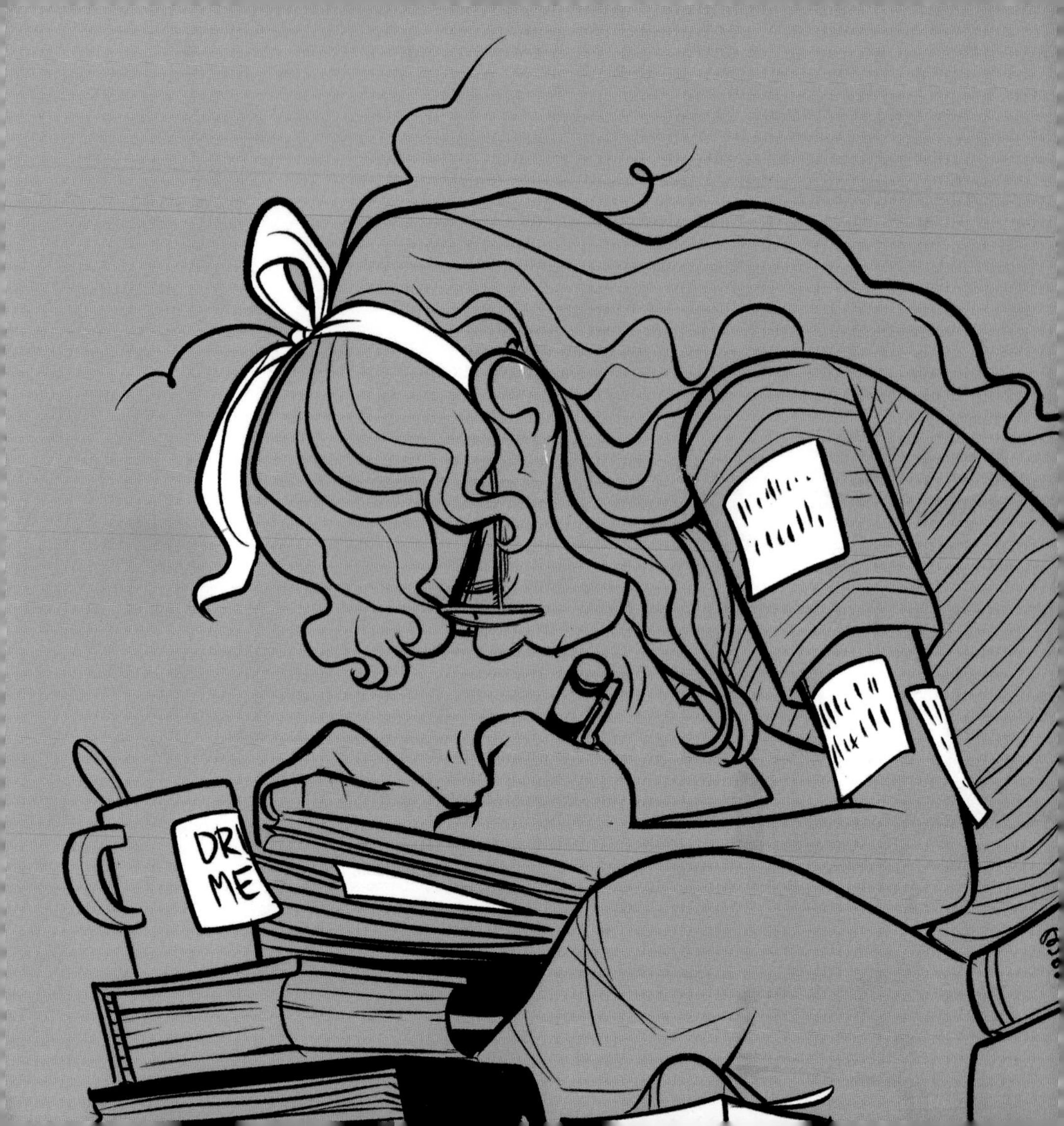
DR
ME

25%
LEARNING

The Hallowed Halls of Academia

"THIS IS THE LIBRARY!
GOOD FOR BOOKS!
BAD FOR PEOPLE WHO
HATE BOOKS."

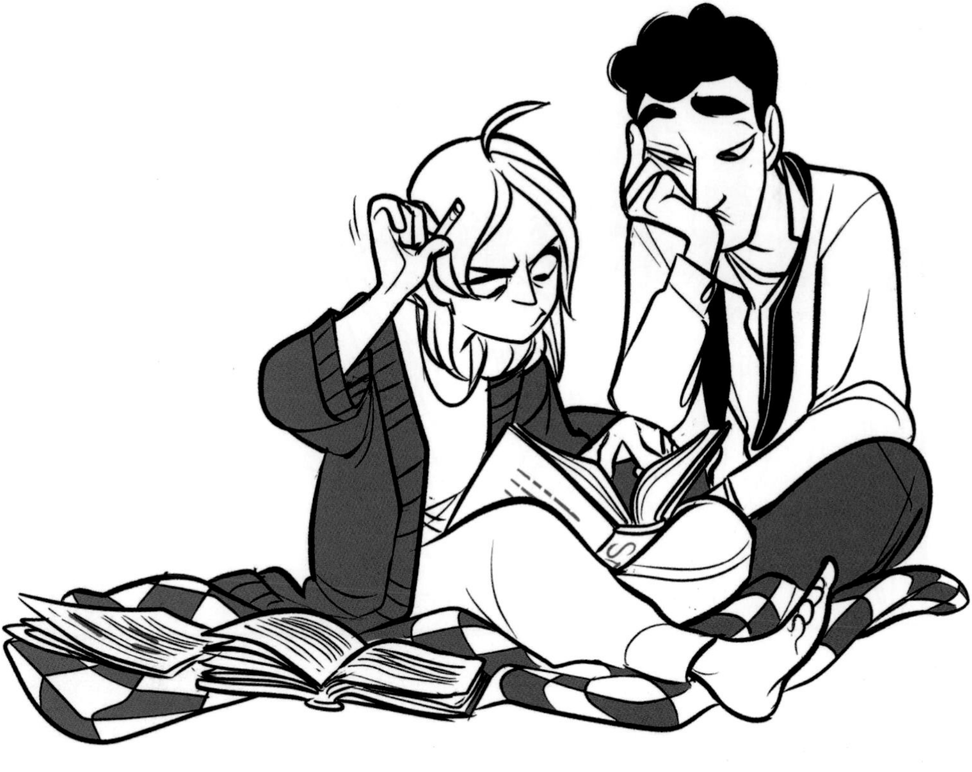

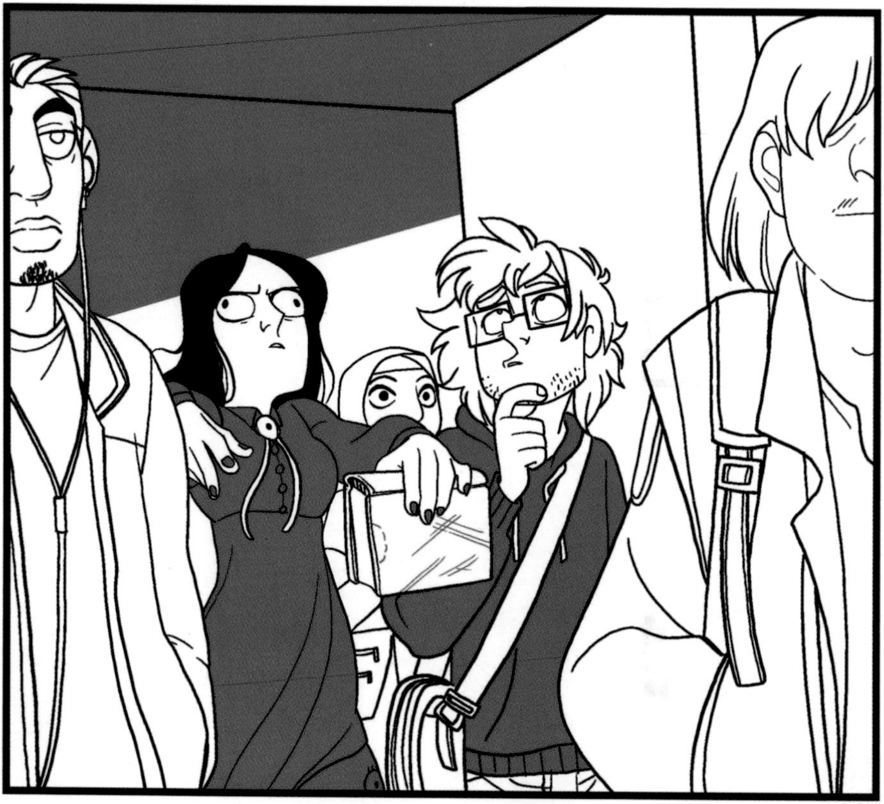

"IF I LIVE THROUGH THIS,
I'M GOING TO CHANGE, ED.
AND IF I DIE IN THE PROCESS,
I'M GOING TO HAUNT PEOPLE
SO THEY DON'T MAKE MY
REVISION MISTAKES."

"I'M NOT...**CERTAIN** THAT
POLTERGEIST ACTIVITY HELPS
PEOPLE CONCENTRATE."

"ESTHER, YOUR MARKS ARE BASED ON ESSAYS YOU HANDED IN FULL OF WAFTY GOTHIC THOUGHTS. IF YOU GET SOMETHING WRONG, IT'S POSSIBLE SOMEONE MAY **SIGH DEEPLY** BEFORE MOVING ON WITH THEIR DAY."

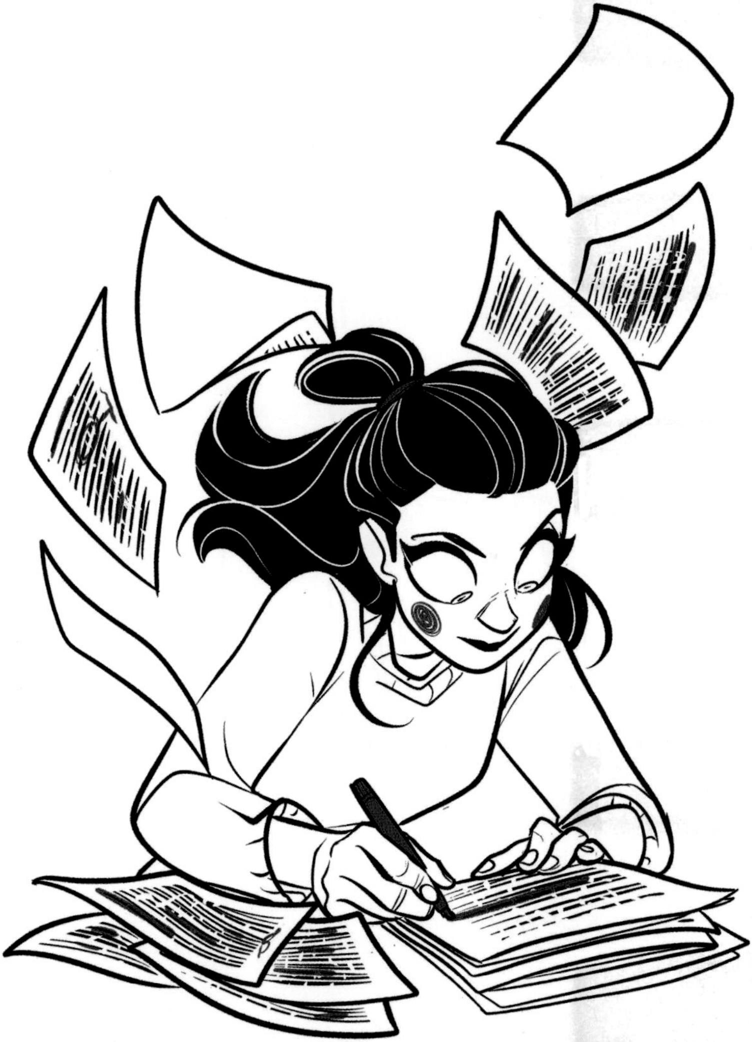

"THAT'S RIGHT, DR. KERMODE,
STARE THE LEARNING INTO ME."

"I'M FLYING, I'M FLYING!
TAKE THAT HEDDA GABLER! POW!"

"I'VE NEVER TYPED SO MANY WORDS. I'M IN LOVE WITH WORDS."

"...**THE END**. WAIT, DO YOU WRITE
'THE END' AT THE END OF AN ESSAY?"

"I WISH I'D ACTUALLY READ HEDDA GABLER."

"WHAT DID PEOPLE DO BEFORE THEIR EXAM RESULTS WERE DELIVERED ELECTRONICALLY?"

"INSTEAD OF REFRESHING THE SAME PAGE EVERY THIRTY SECONDS? I GUESS THEY JUST WHIPPED THEMSELVES WITH WET TOWELS."

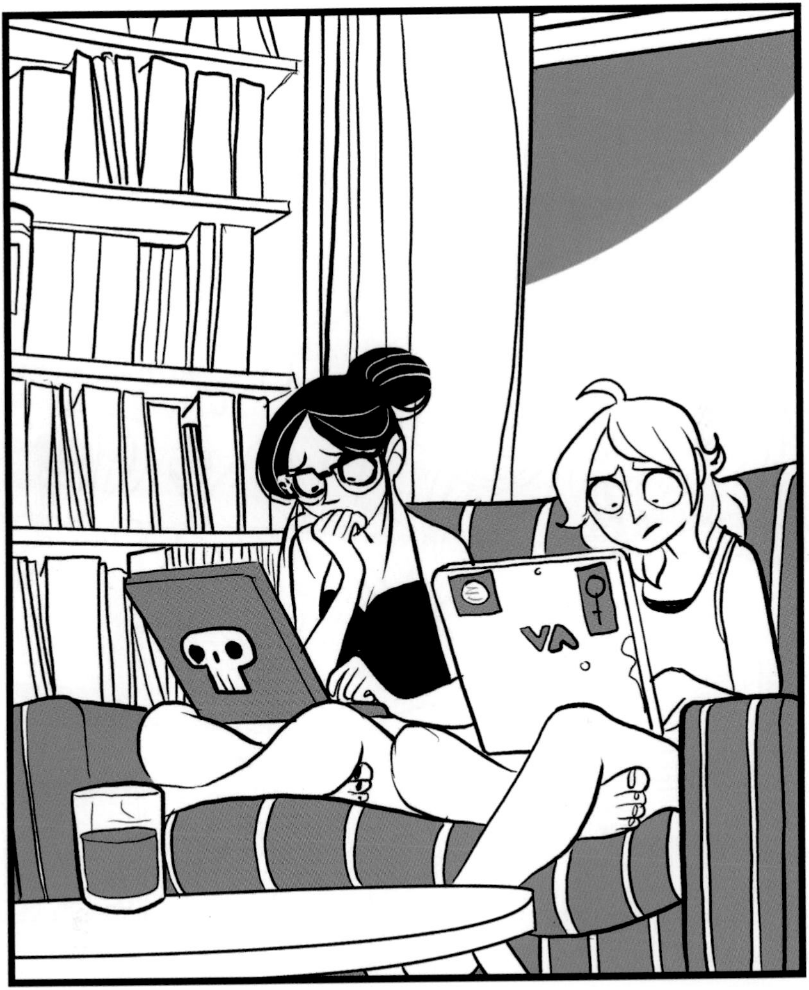

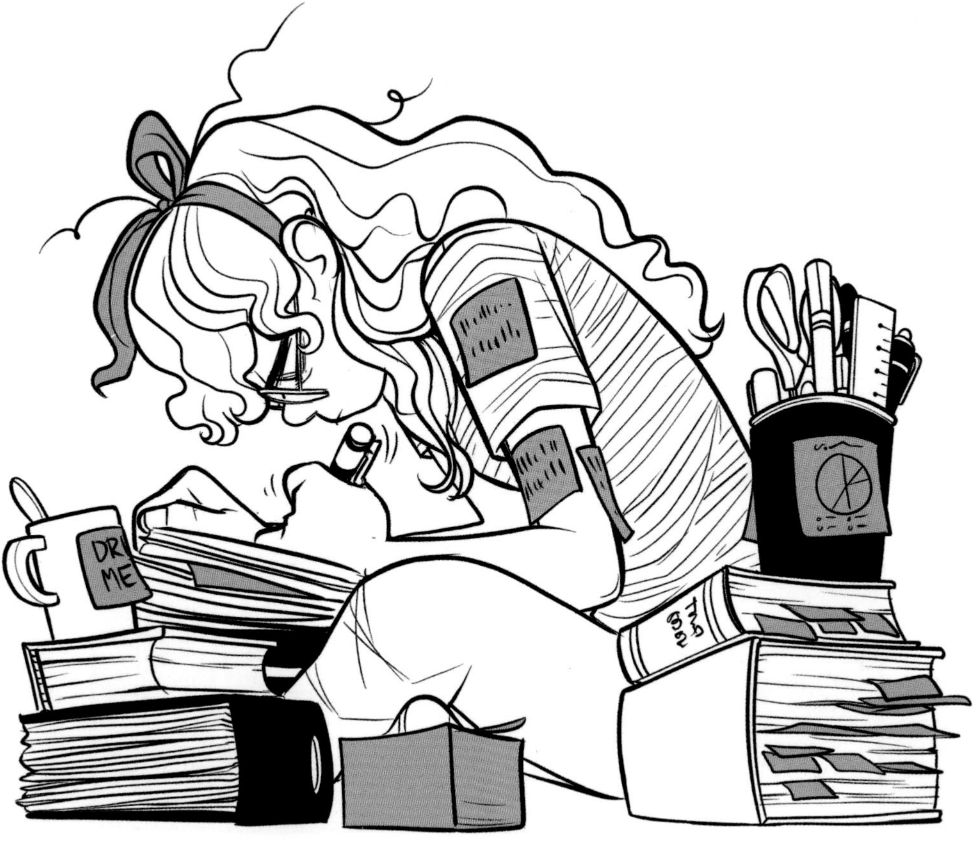
DRI
ME

"I HAVE A SYSTEM. I MAKE DETAILED REVISION NOTES, THEN I MAKE THOSE INTO CONCENTRATED REVISION NOTES, THEN I TRY TO GET IT DOWN TO TWO FLASH CARDS OR A DIAGRAM. IF I HAVE TIME I MAKE A **MEMORY PALACE!**"

"THIS IS A WONDERFUL GLIMPSE INTO A PARALLEL UNIVERSE WHERE EVERY DECISION IS THE EXACT OPPOSITE OF THE ONE I TOOK. I'M HAVING A PANIC ATTACK."

"IT'S A HEARTBREAKING WORK OF STAGGERING GENIUS, ESTHER. BEST DISSERTATION EVER. IN MANY WAYS IT SUPERSEDES THE NEED TO READ ANY OF THE GREAT AMERICAN NOVELS."

"REALLY?"

"NO, BUT THE SPELLING AND GRAMMAR WERE TOP-DRAWER."

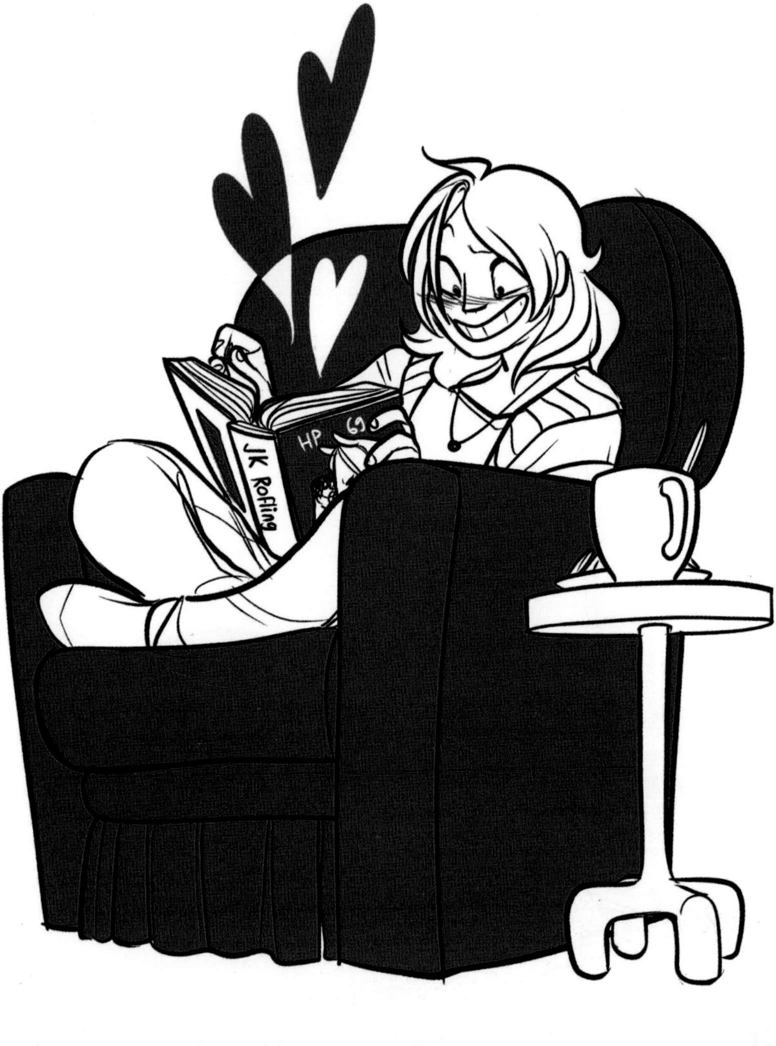
JK Rofling
HP 69

"I UNDERSTAND ROMANTIC POETRY. THERE'S NOTHING I DON'T KNOW ABOUT THE SENSUAL WORLD. I'M ON TOP OF MY HORNY STYLISTICS!"

"I SORT OF WISH I'D STUCK WITH SCIENCE. FUNNY HOW WE LET A SIXTEEN-YEAR-OLD MAKE THE DECISIONS FOR OUR ADULT SELVES."

"I MEAN, YOU WOULDN'T LET A MONKEY DRIVE A COMMUTER TRAIN, WOULD YOU?"

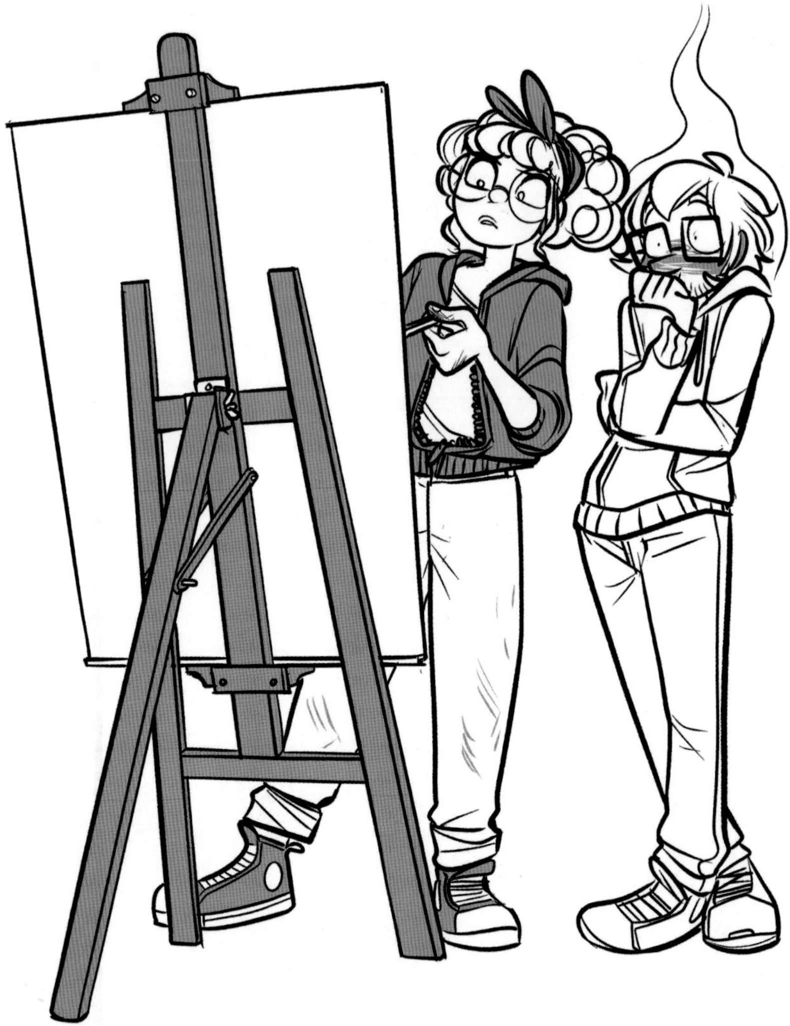

"I'M NOT SURE ABOUT BURLESQUE LIFE DRAWING. TOO SAUCY."

"I THINK THESE ARE GOOD FOR A BEGINNER. THERE'S DEFINITELY A SENSE THAT YOU WITNESSED SOMETHING."

"IT TURNS
OUT CONSTANT PANIC
IS GREAT CARDIO."

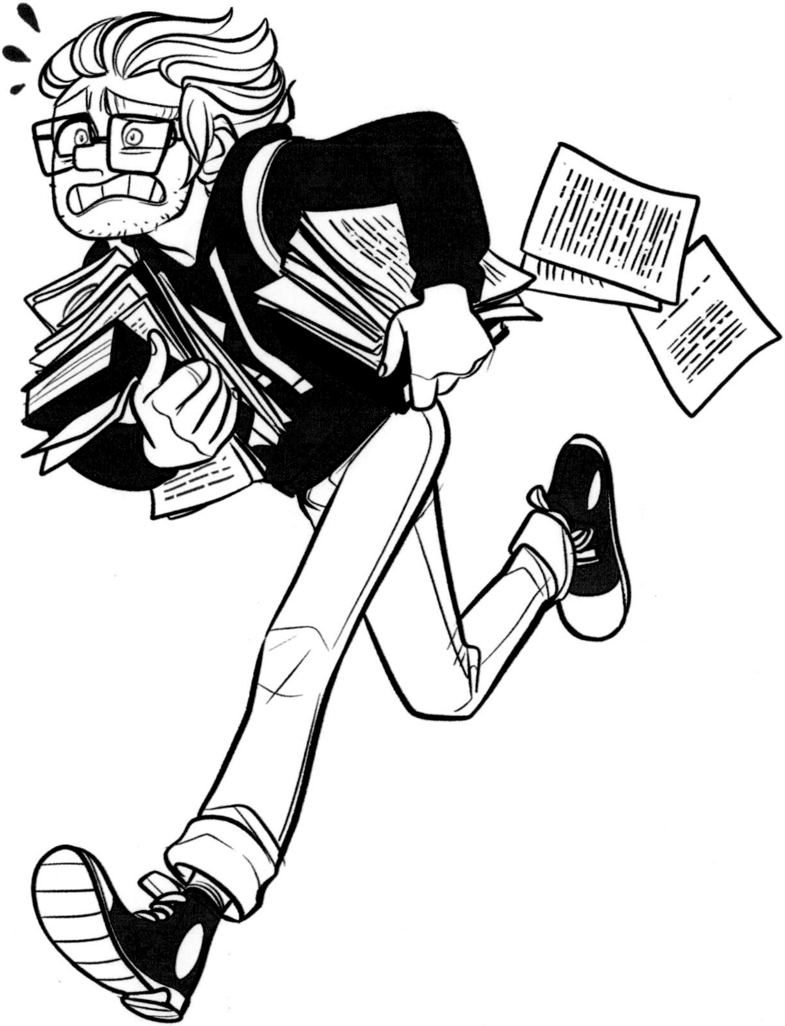

"I'VE SEEN SO MANY BEAUTIFUL THINGS TODAY. I HAVE TO GET A GOOD JOB SO I CAN BUY ALL THE THINGS."

"CAN I GET A GOOD JOB WITH AN ENGLISH LITERATURE DEGREE?"

"OF COURSE YOU CAN. BUT THE TWO THINGS WON'T BE IN ANY WAY RELATED."

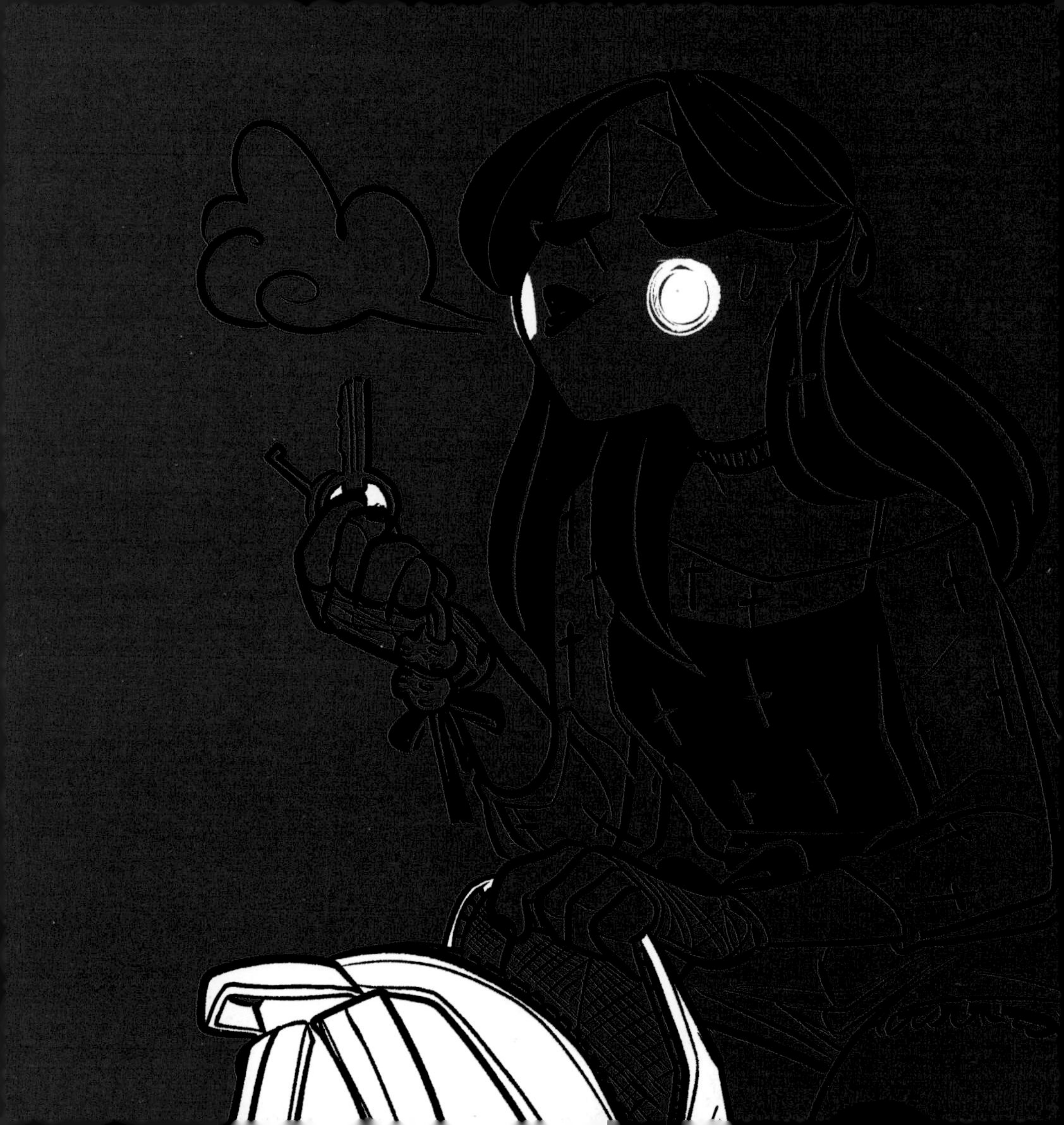

25%
EARNING

The World of Work

"LOOK, I AM GOING TO GO IN THERE AND TWERK FURIOUSLY FOR YOU. AND BY TWERK, I MEAN 'NETWORK,' THAT IS THE NEW NAME FOR IT NOW, GET USED TO IT."

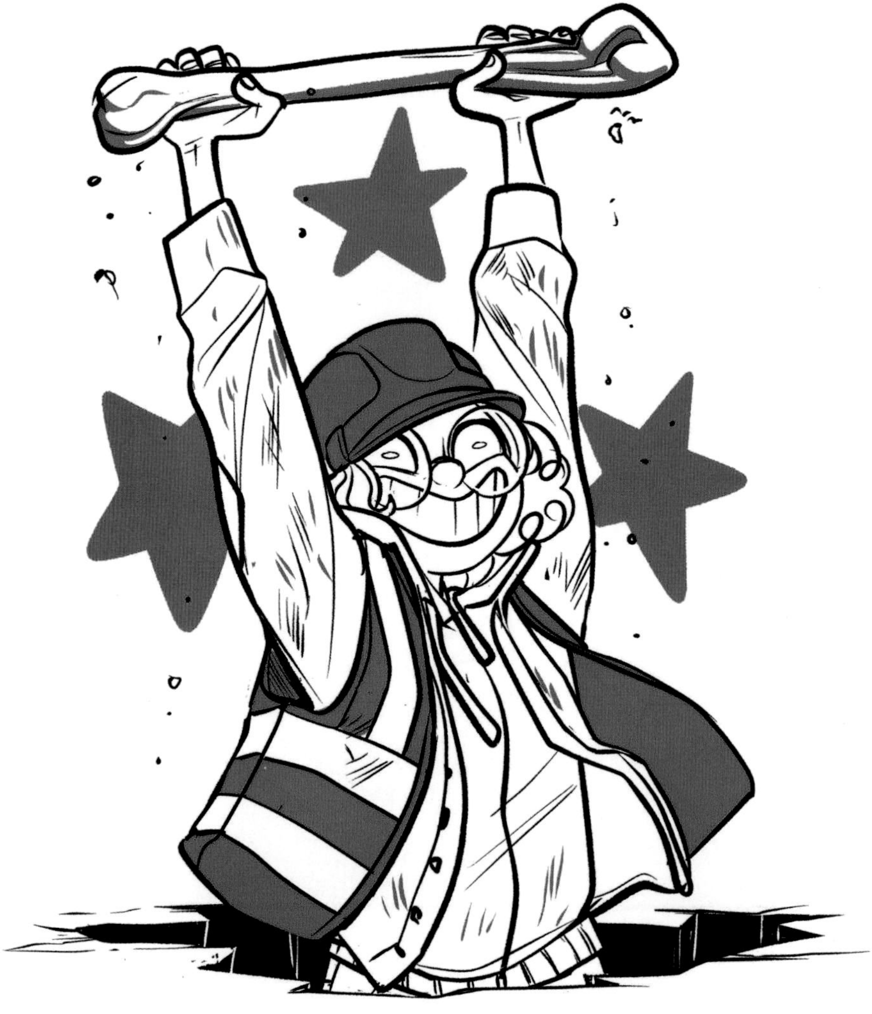

"I KNOW ARCHAEOLOGY
FASHION IS 'SPECIAL'."

"YES, KHAKI COTTON
DRILL KEEPS THE CURSES
AWAY. THE EXTRA POCKETS
INTIMIDATE GHOSTS."

"OH YES! DO THEY PAY?
I NEED HOT CASH."

"UH, I THINK DOING THINGS
FOR FREE IS AT THE HEART
OF 'VOLUNTEERING'."

"WHEN THE GOING GETS TOUGH, YOU JUST HAVE TO REMEMBER THE HIPPOCRATIC OATH: *'I'M LOVIN' IT'.*"

"NOW LET'S GET IN THERE AND FIND SOME OPPORTUNITIES. AND IF WE CAN'T FIND OPPORTUNITIES, WE'LL GET OUR MONEY'S WORTH IN COCKTAILS."

"IF IT ALL GOES SIDEWAYS, I'LL JUST ROB A LOAD OF THE BANK MONEY AND LEG IT."

"APPARENTLY THE WORLD OF WORK IS SAYING YOU'RE PASSIONATE ABOUT THINGS... THAT NO ONE IN THEIR RIGHT MIND WOULD BE PASSIONATE ABOUT!"

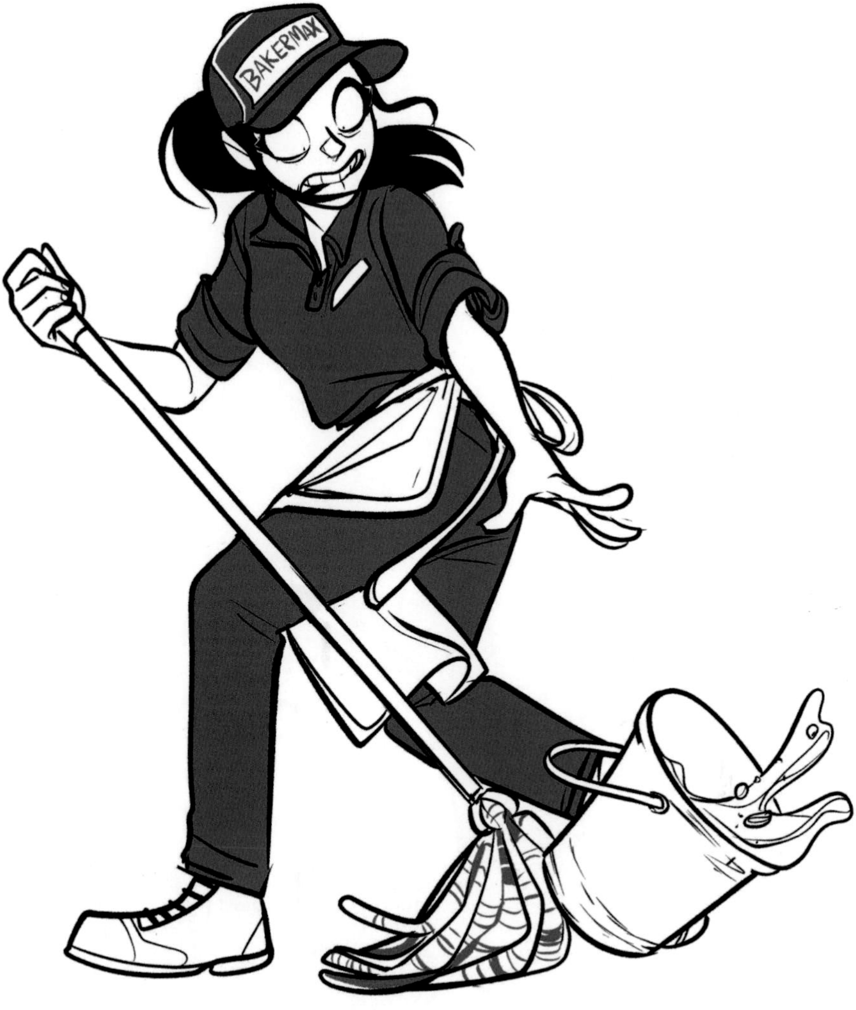
BAKERMAX

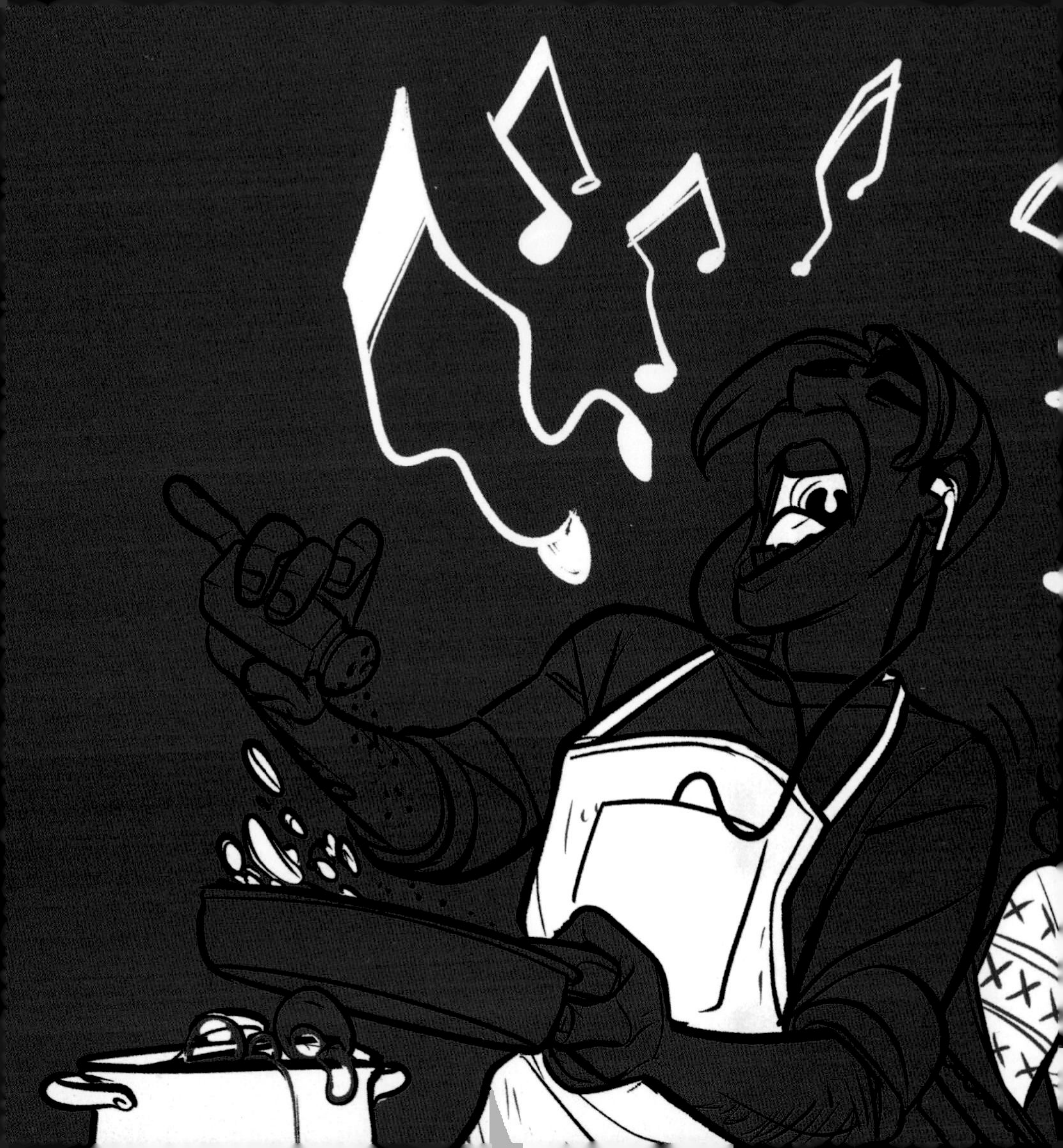

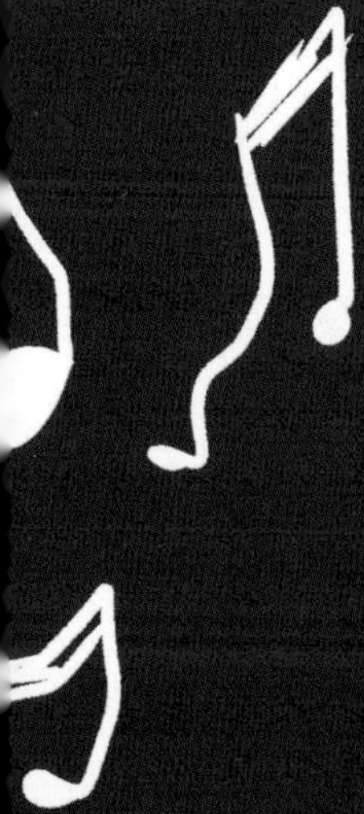

25%
BURNING NIGHTS OF EROTIC PASSION

The Realm of Romance

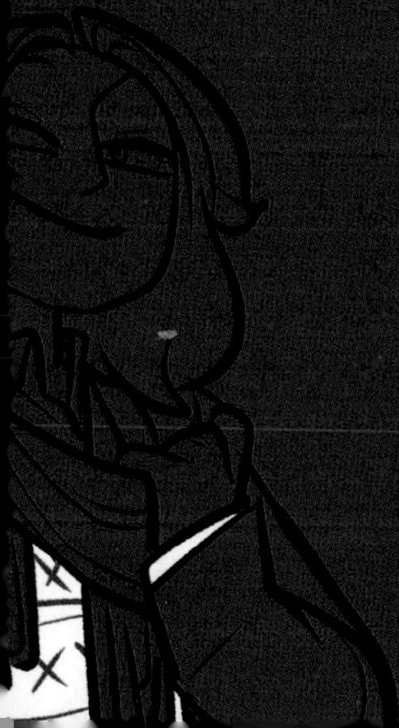

"I MAY NEVER LOVE AGAIN."

"OH, YOU WILL!
YOU WILL! TRY LOVING
SOMETHING SMALL FIRST.
LIKE A PAPERCLIP."

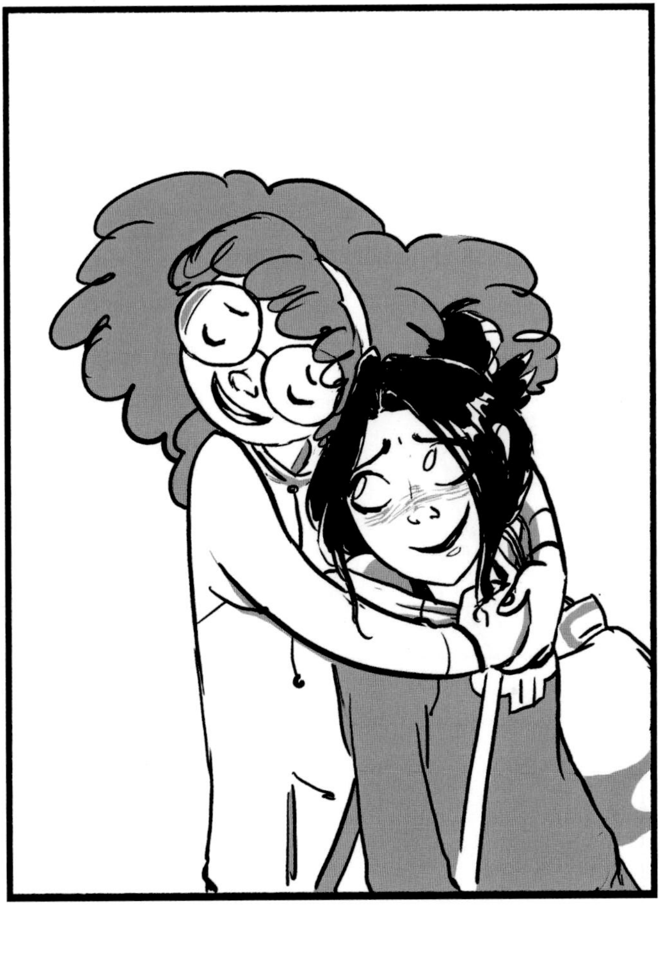

"UNREQUITED LOVE
IS A BAD PATH. IT'S CALLED
A CRUSH BECAUSE IT
CRUSHES YOU."

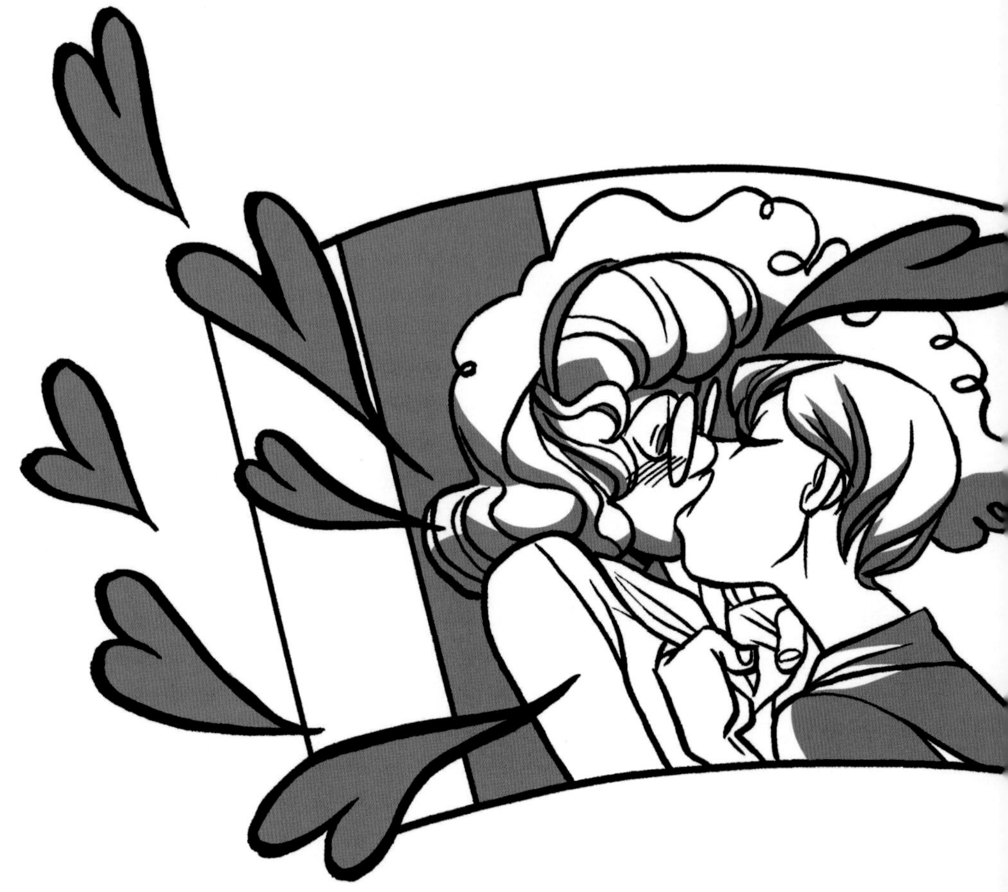

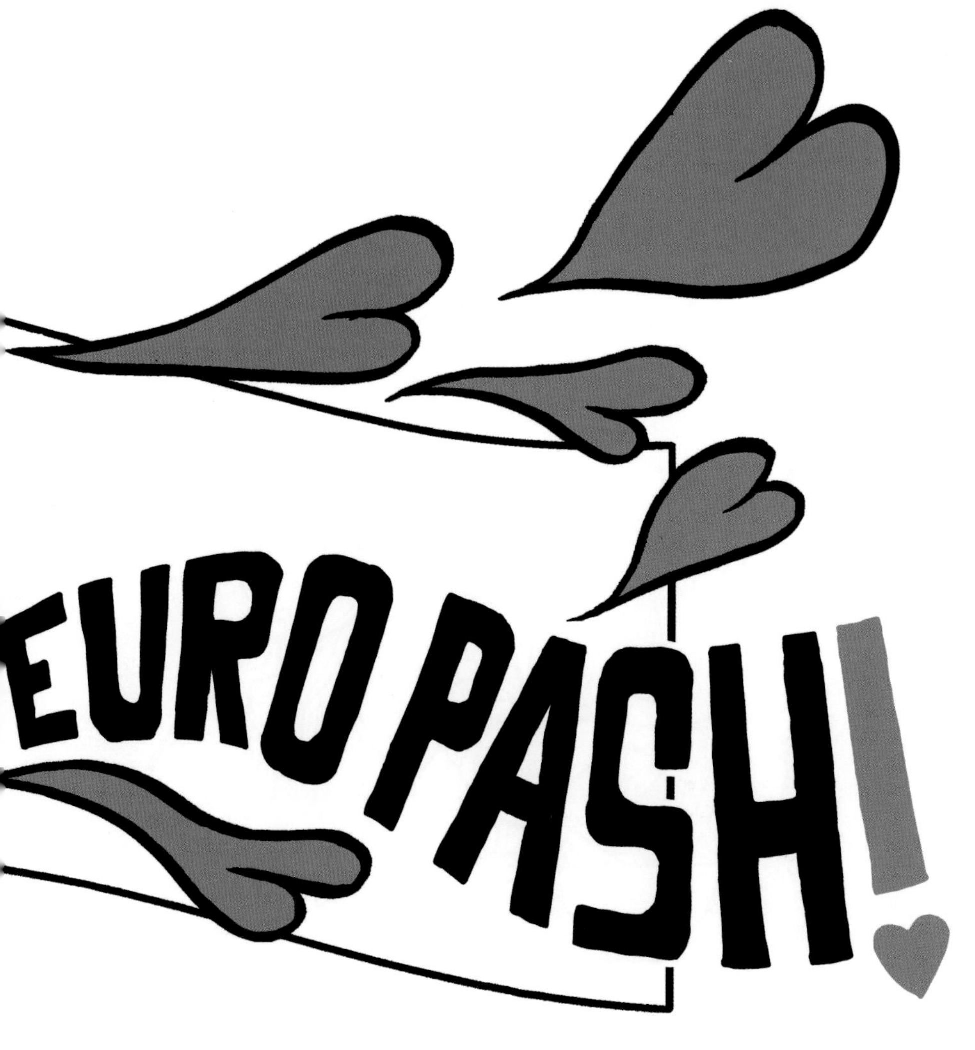
EURO PASH!

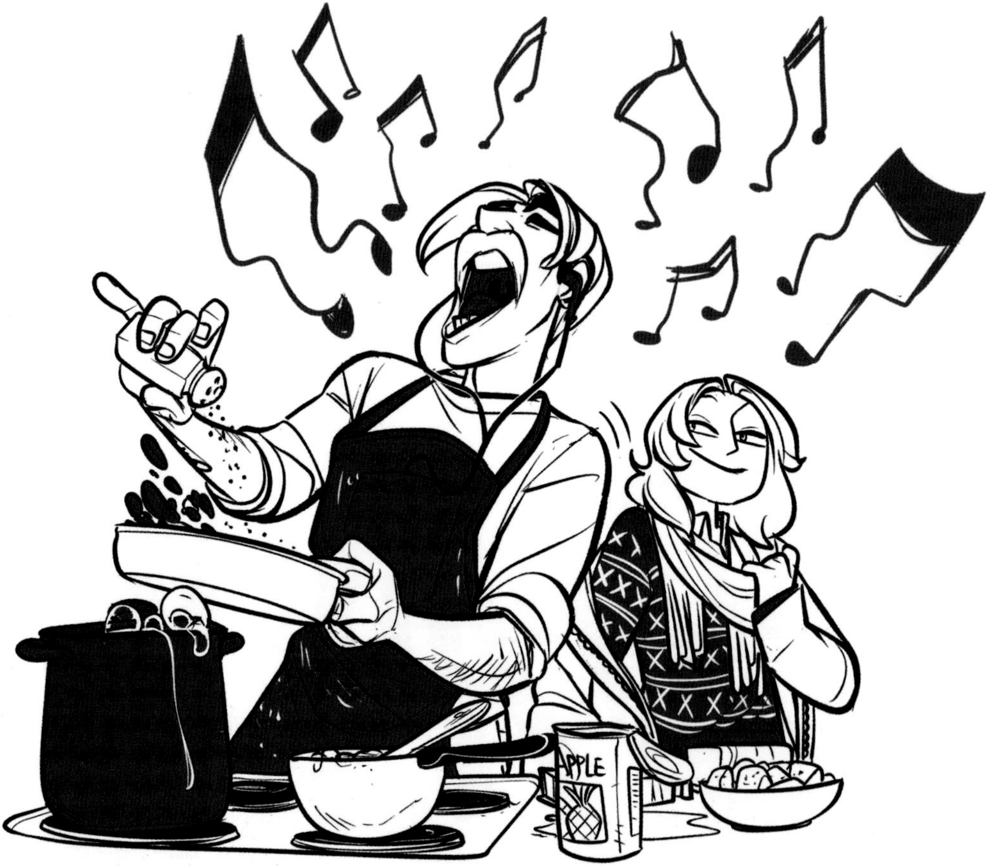
APPLE

"I'VE MADE A
TRULY **GARF-WORTHY**
LASAGNA."

"OH MY MAN,
MY SPECIAL MAN."

"HOW WAS YOUR DATE?
ARE YOU **IN LERV?**"

"SHE'S INSANE.
AND I THINK I MIGHT
BE IN **LUST**. THE CURE
IS **BREAKFAST**."

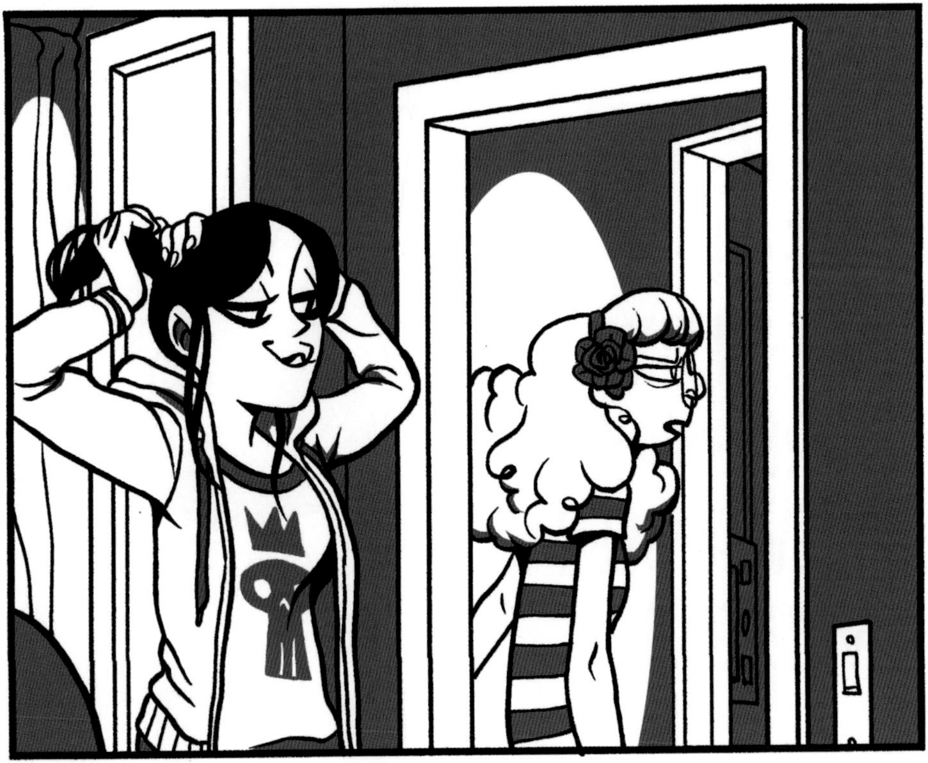

"THIS IS THE FIRST NAIL-BITING THREE-WAY I'VE EVER BEEN INVOLVED IN."

"I HEAR THERE ARE SOHO SEX DUNGEONS DEDICATED JUST TO NAIL-BITING THREE-WAYS. QUITE NICHE."

"ALL THAT **FUSS** OVER ESTHER'S BOY. HE DIDN'T SEEM ALL THAT GREAT."

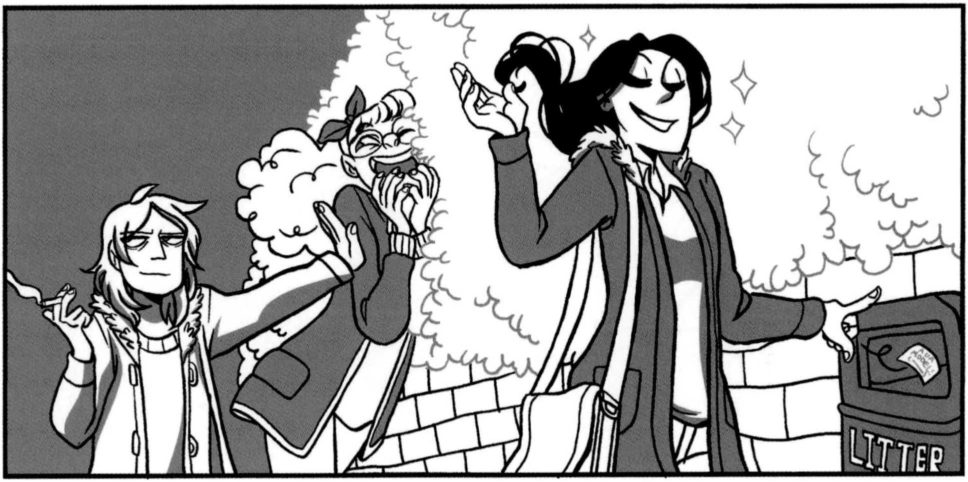
LITTER

"MEN MEN MEN
MEN MEN. THE MEN OF
THE PAST, CONSUMING VITAL
FEMININE BANDWIDTH."

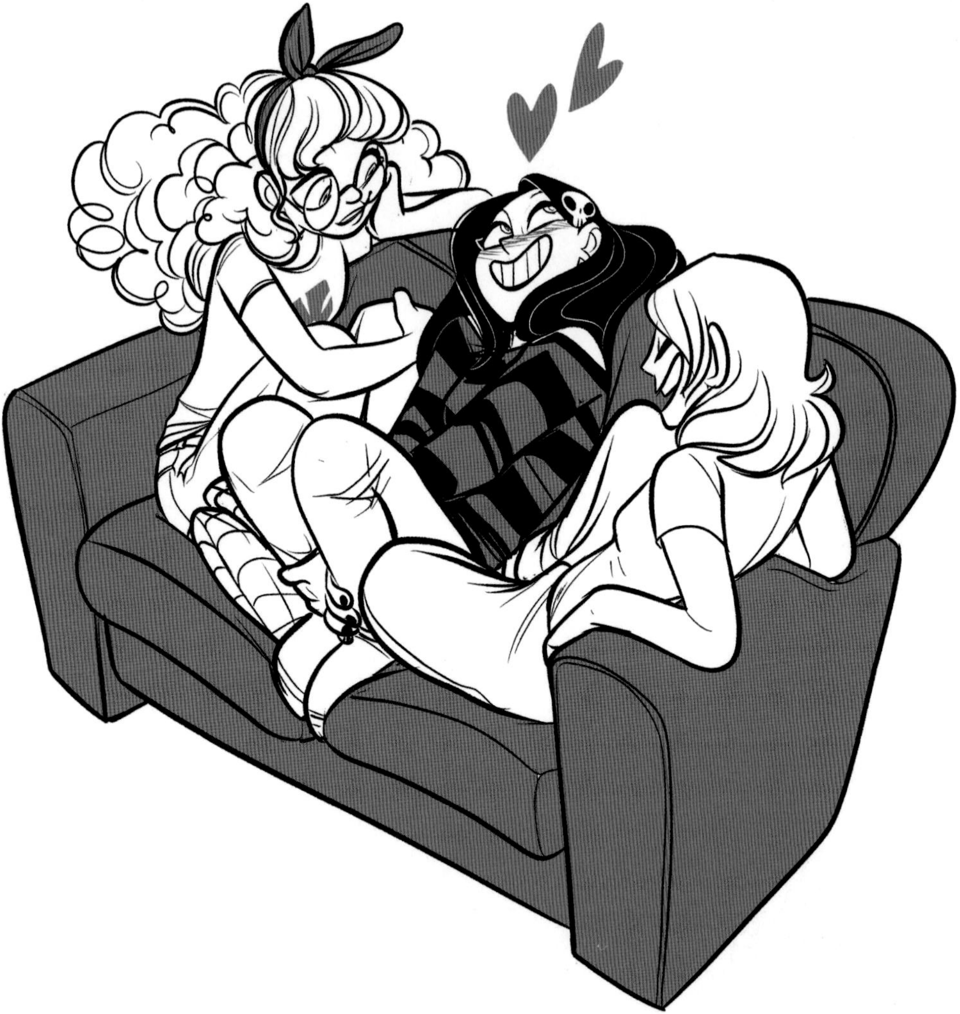

"HOW DID YOU
KNOW YOU LIKED BOYS?"

"WHEN I WAS FOURTEEN,
MY BRAIN OPENED UP A WHOLE
NEW WING DEDICATED TO FEELING
HORNY ABOUT THEM."

"LISTEN, JUST KISS
BOTH KINDS OF FACE.
MAYBE YOU'LL ENJOY
THEM EQUALLY. THAT'S FINE.
LET LOVE RULE. IT'S THE '90S,
GET USED TO IT."

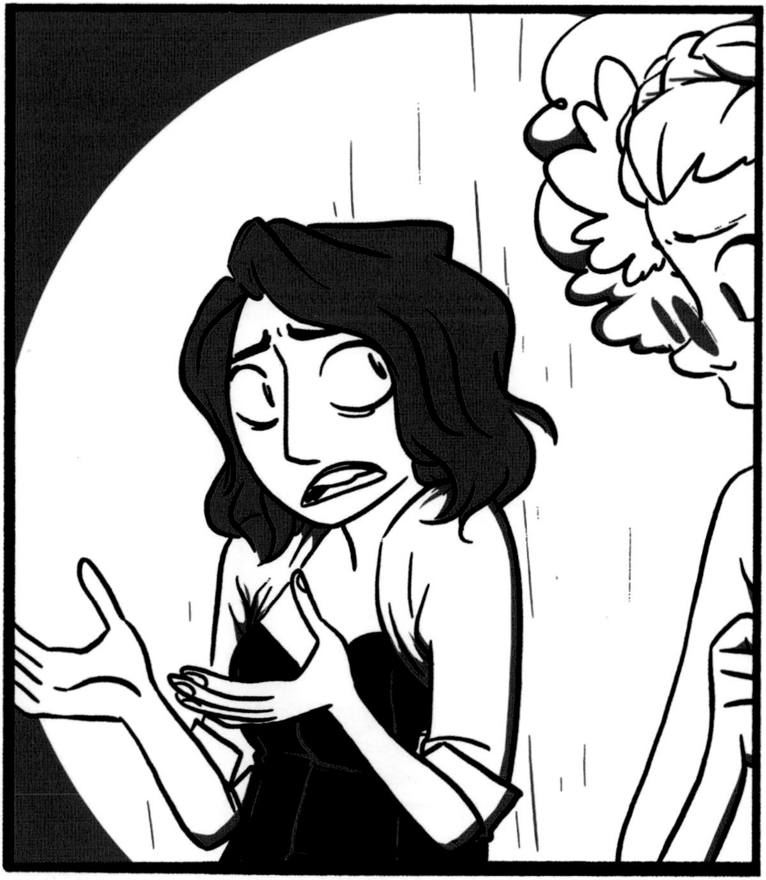

"WELCOME TO THE BAD SEX CLUB, YOU BIG FOOL. POPULATION: EVERYONE WHO EVER DID THE DEED."

"I MADE YOU
A LITTLE LUNCH! IT'S
YOUR PRIZE FOR BEING
SEXY AND NICE."

"IS THAT A SNACK-SIZE
BAG OF M&MS? I'M A
LUCKY LADY!"

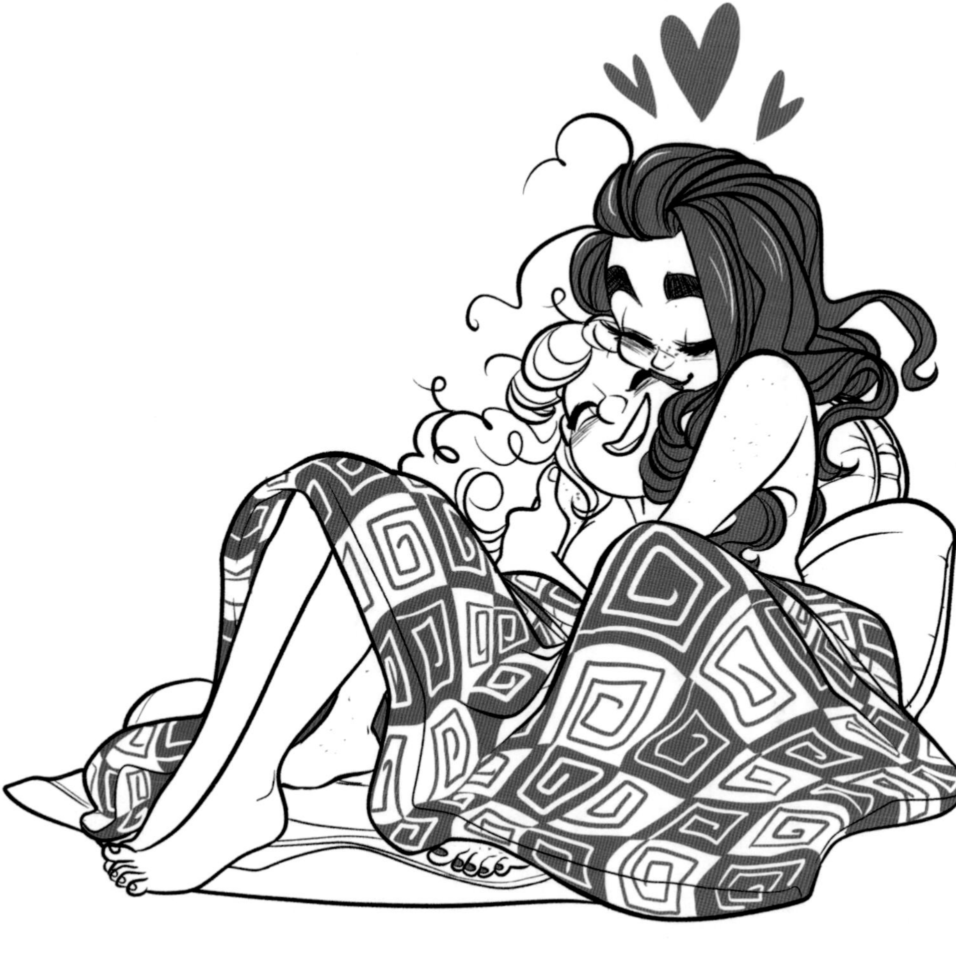

"IMAGINE A LARGE BODY OF WATER. IN IT ARE MANY GILLED CREATURES. ESTHER IS BUT ONE OF THOSE. MANY OTHERS ARE VIABLE."

"ARE YOU TELLING ME TO MAKE LOVE TO A MERMAID? BECAUSE I BLOODY WELL WOULD."

"I CAN'T BREAK UP WITH HER...**BUT I MUST!**"

"GOOD GOOD, THAT'S YOUR MANTRA. APPLY IT RUTHLESSLY."

"I HAVE! THOSE ARE THE ONLY THOUGHTS I'VE HAD FOR THE LAST TWO WEEKS!"

"I FEEL INCREDIBLE!"

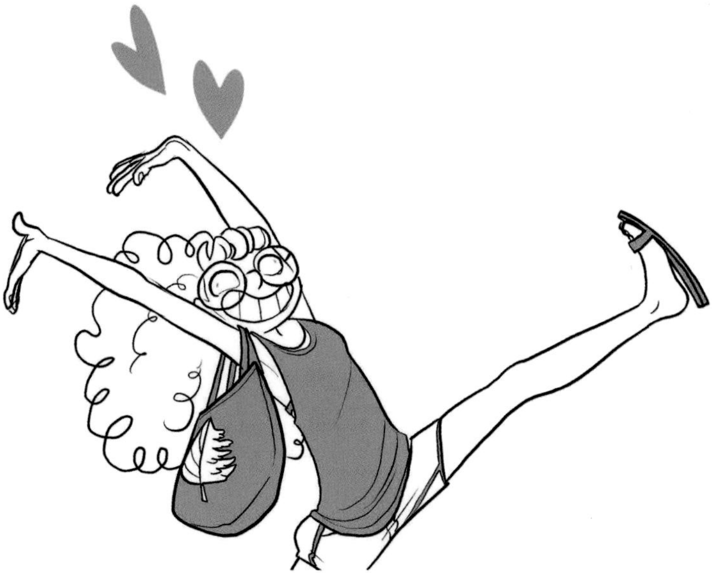

"I FEEL TERRIBLE!"

"YOU KNOW WHAT YOUR PROBLEM IS? BAD GIRLS ARE YOUR KRYPTONITE."

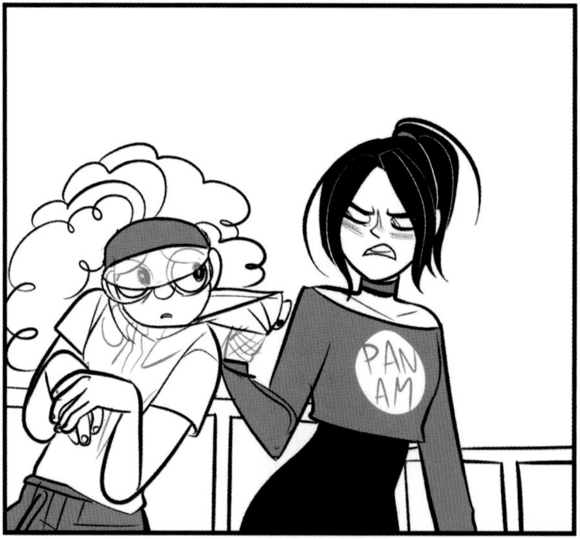
PAN AM

"THEY JUST NEED SHOWING HOW TO BE GOOD!"

"SUSAN PTOLEMY IS A POWERFUL AND COMPLICATED WOMAN, BUT WE EXIST IN HARMONY. I'M THERE FOR WHEN SHE PERCEIVES THE WORLD AS A TERRIBLE RED MIST. SHE'S THERE FOR WHEN I JIGSAW MY FINGERS OFF."

"SOMETIMES A LADY
LOVES A LADY AND-"

"I UNDERSTAND **LESBIANS**, DAISY!
ELLEN DEGENERES!"

"BUT BEING LESBIANS MUST BE **AMAZING** BECAUSE **THIS** IS MAD."

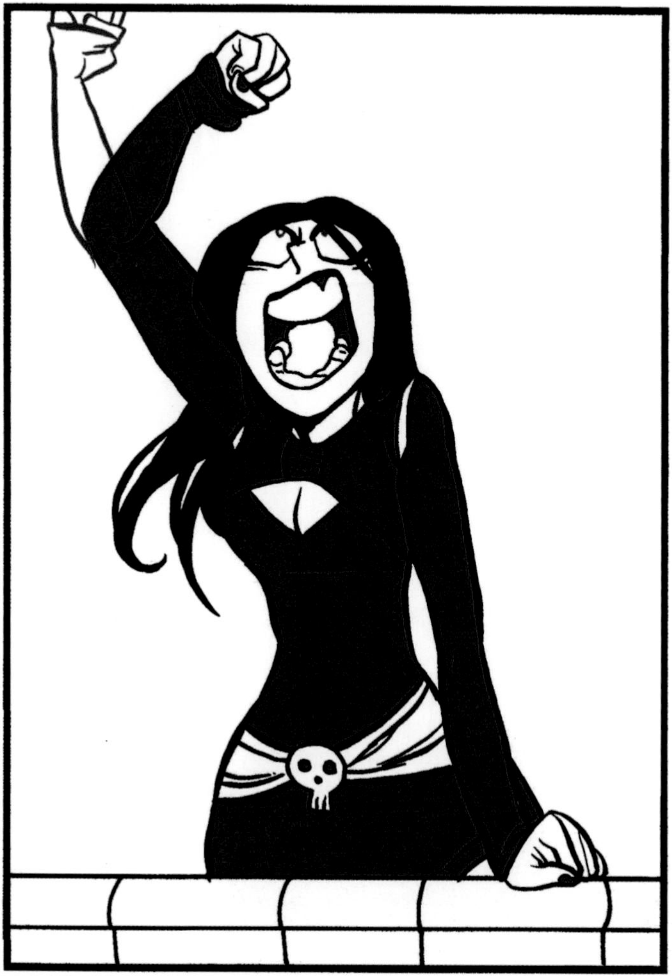

"HOW AM I MEANT TO
GET BACK ON THE ROMANCE HORSE
IF IT DOESN'T HAVE A SADDLE?
MUST I GO BAREBACK?
MUST I BREAK HIM?"

"I DIDN'T THINK IT WAS POSSIBLE TO BE DRUNK OF OTHER PEOPLE'S SEXUAL TENSION!"

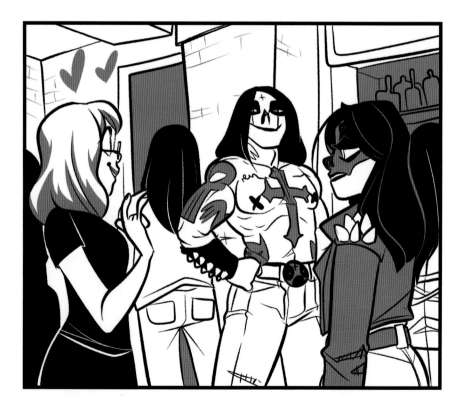

"UGH, I WOULD NEVER
DATE A BLACK METALLER.
ONLY ROOM FOR ONE CORPSE
AT MY VANITY UNIT."

"I AM VERY HORNY ABOUT THIS AWFUL SITUATION."

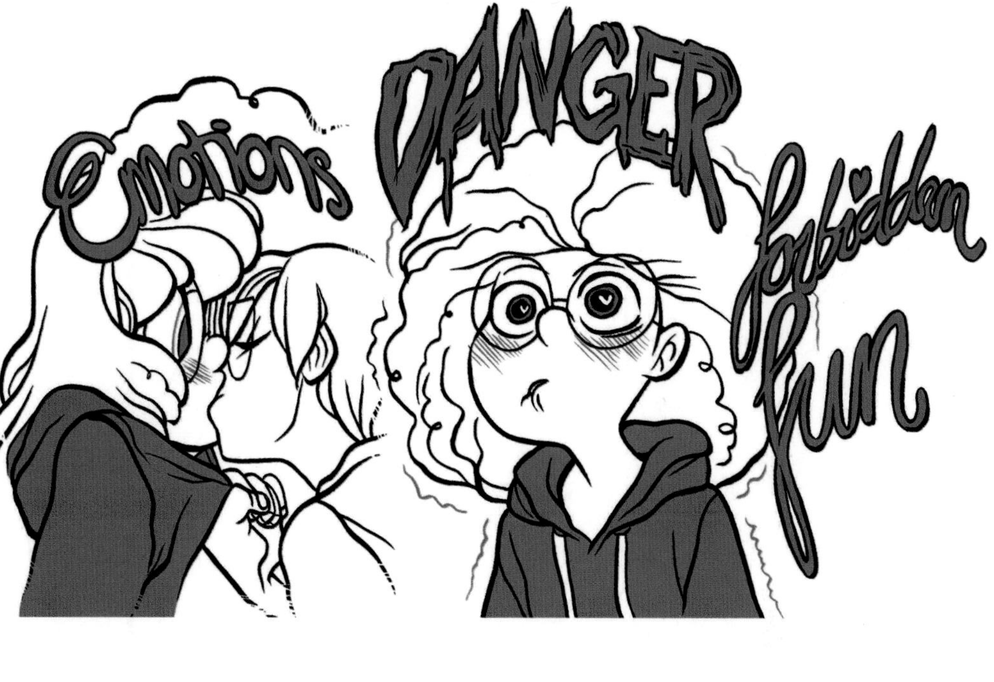
Emotions
DANGER
forbidden
fun

"'GET YOURSELF OUT THERE!'
IS JUST A THING PEOPLE SAY.
IT'S LIKE A 2000 PIECE JIGSAW
WITH NO PICTURE ON THE BOX."

"I THINK YOUR LIFE
IS LIKE A GARDEN.
YOU HAVE TO LOOK
AFTER IT."

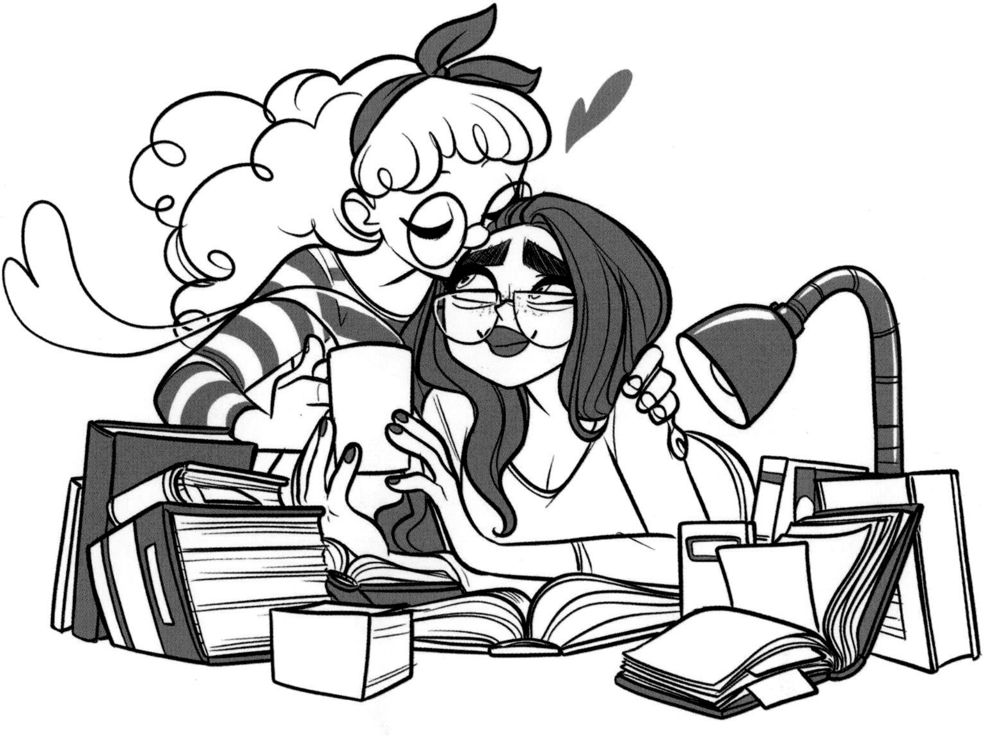

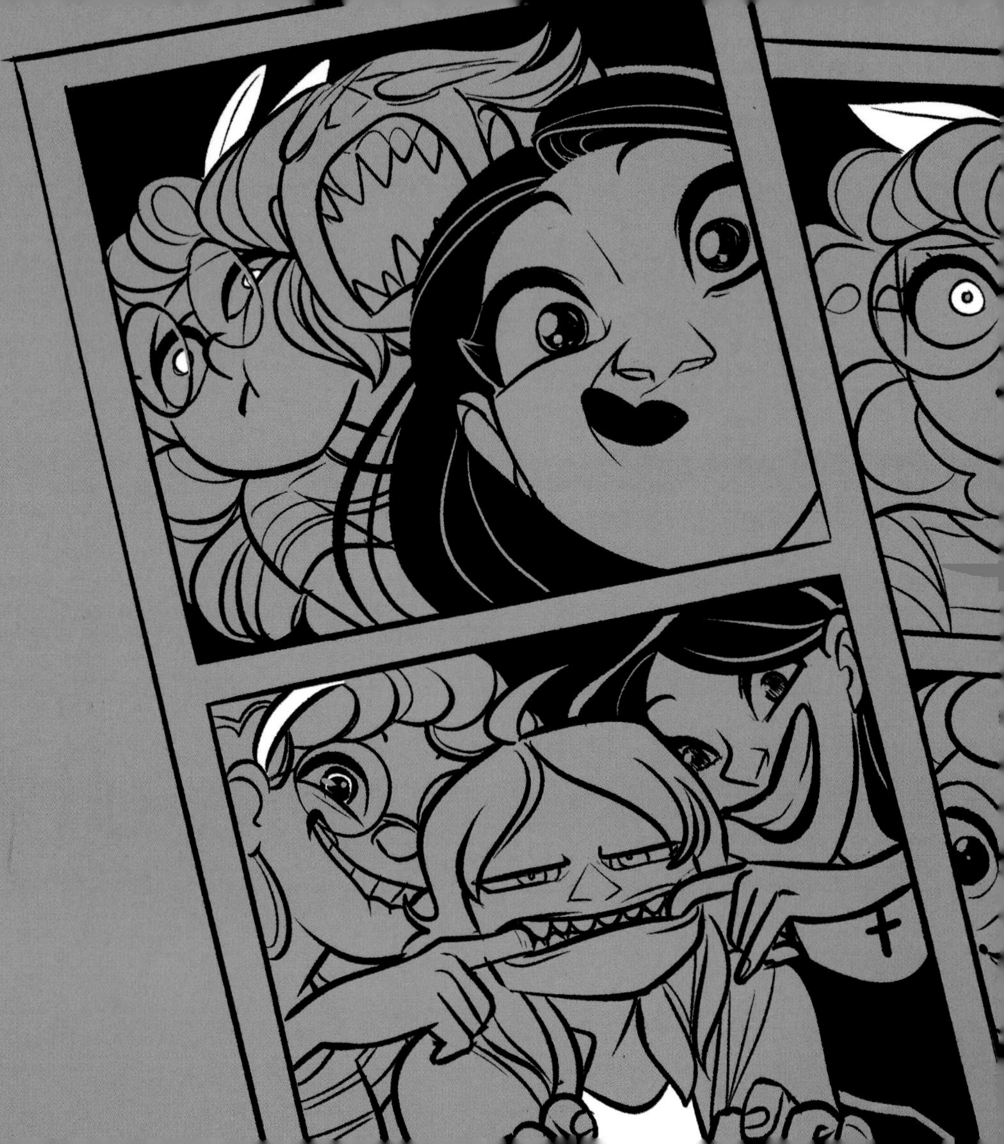

25%
TURNING
STRANGERS
INTO BFFS

The Unbreakable Bonds of Friendship

"ONLY ONE PERSON CAN TRULY UNDERSTAND ME AND IT'S NOT **YOU**, FLOOR."

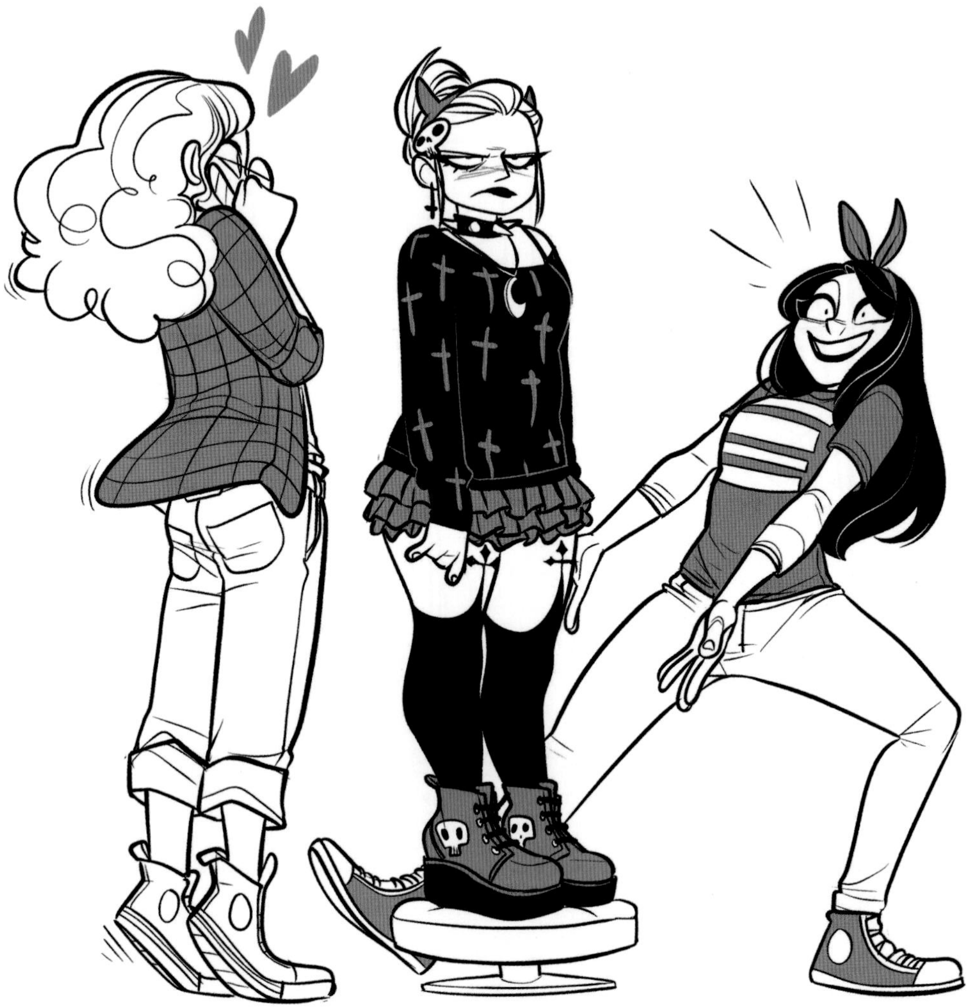

"SUSAN, YOU ARE A **BEAUTIFUL LADY** WITH ARMS LIKE CANNONS, LEGS LIKE PISTONS AND A FINE HEAD OF HAIR."

"IF YOUR FREAK FLAG
IS A PICTURE OF YOU GOING
TO BED AT NINE-THIRTY
AND READING, GO FOR IT.
FLY IT HIGH."

"HOW COME WHENEVER WE TEST YOUR UNDERWORLD CREDENTIALS, YOU END UP IN MORTAL DANGER?"

"HAVE YOU NEVER READ ANY RAYMOND CHANDLER? THE HERO GETS BEATEN UP ON **EVERY PAGE!**"

"OH I SEE. YOU TWO ARE HAVING AN AFFAIR. WELL, DON'T MIND ME, I'VE ONLY BEEN **SAVING LIVES**."

"OH SUSAN. HE WON'T EVEN LET ME PUT EYELINER ON HIM JUST TO SEE WHAT IT WOULD LOOK LIKE...LET ALONE MAKE SPORT WITH HIS BODY."

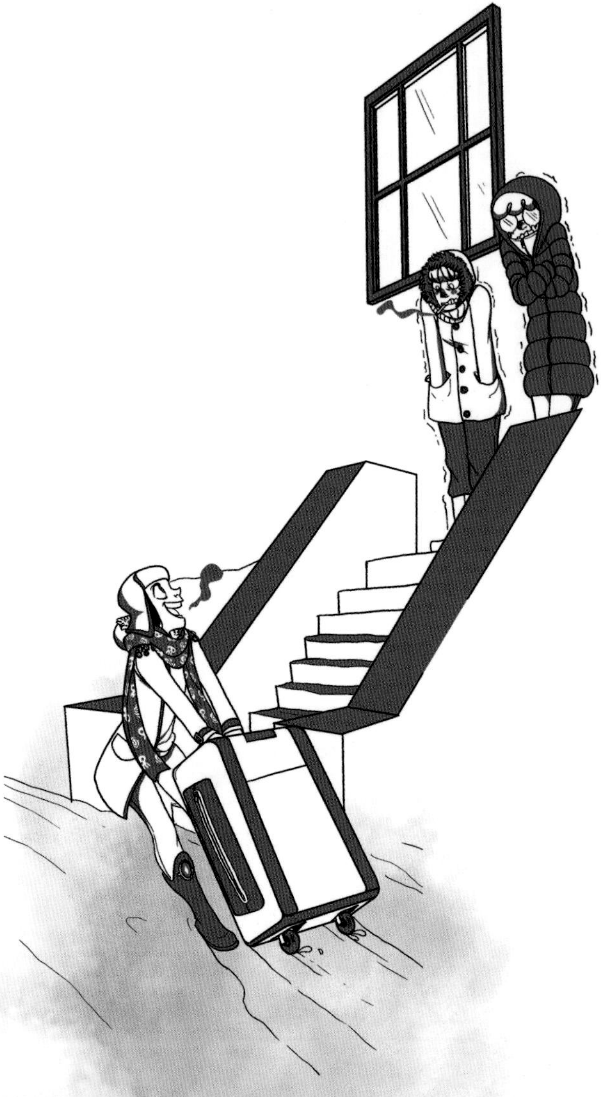

"YOU'RE WAITING
FOR ME! IN THE COLD!
THIS IS THE KIND OF SLAVISH
DEVOTION I'M INTO."

"ISN'T THIS THE KIND OF INFANTILE CAPER SUSAN AND DAISY USUALLY HELP YOU WITH?"

NO, McGRAW, I NEED A PRACTICAL BOY! **NOT A COTERIE OF FLIBBERTIGIBBETS!"**

"ESTHER, WE LOVE YOU. WHO WOULDN'T? THAT BIG BEAUTIFUL FACE, LIKE A SEXY MOON."

"I CAN'T BELIEVE
I FOUND PEOPLE WILLING
TO DO A JIGSAW PUZZLE OF A
HORSE WITH ME FOR THREE
HOURS AT A PARTY!"

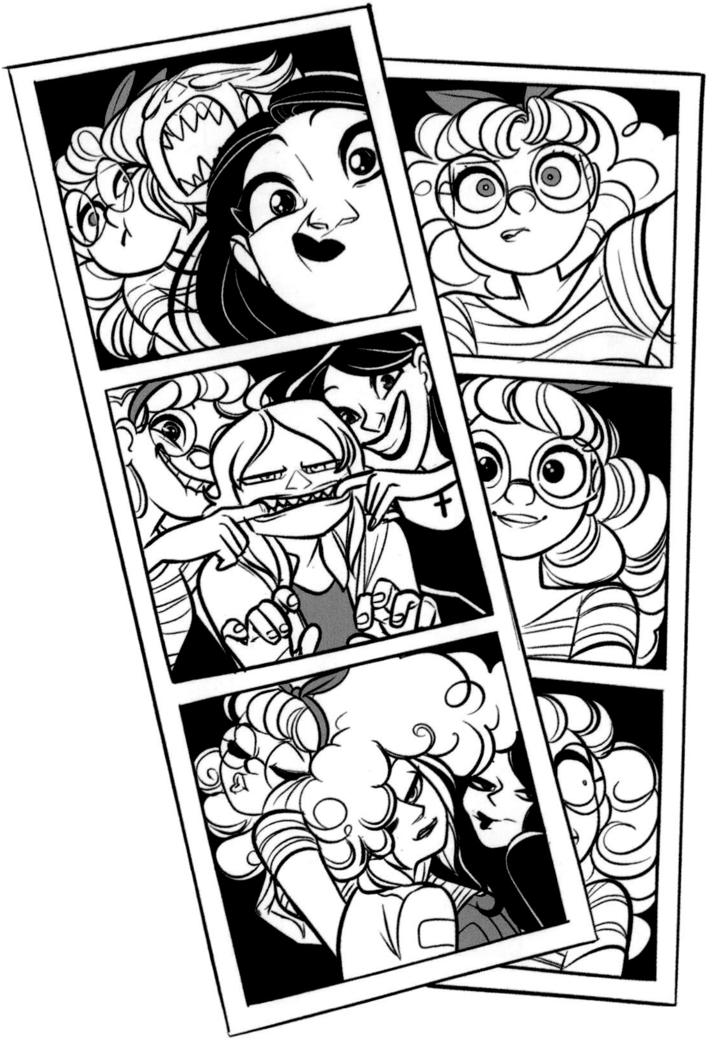

"TWO'S LESBIANS,
THREE'S A COVEN,
AND WE DON'T EVEN QUALIFY
AS A COVEN ANYMORE."

"NOTHING IN MY BROWNIE TRAINING HAS PREPARED ME FOR THE LAWLESS WILD WEST OF THE MODERN MUSIC FESTIVAL. IT MADE ME DOUBT MY FRIENDSHIP."

"WITH ESTHER?"

"WITH HUMANITY."

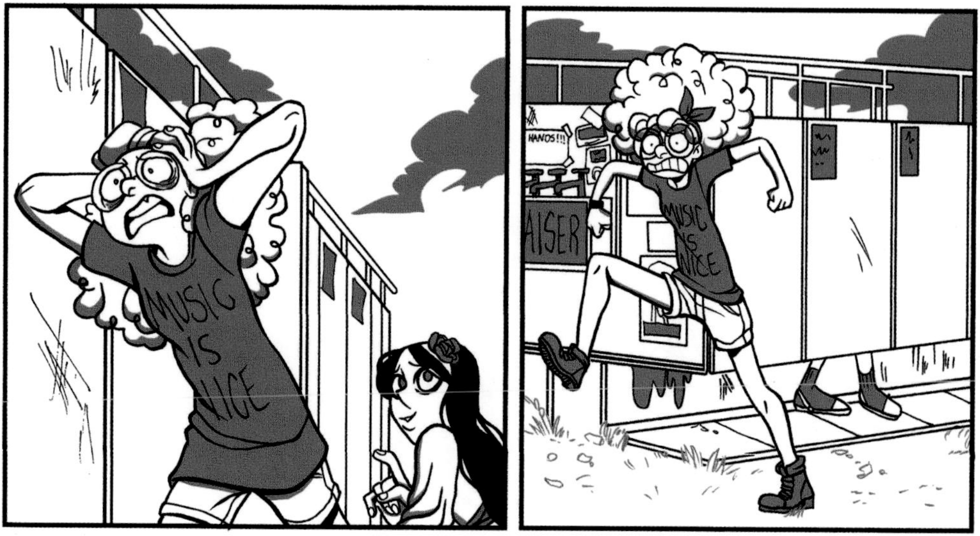
HANDS!!!
AISER

"THINK ABOUT ALL THOSE THINGS YOU LIKE IN THE DAYTIME! FRESH AIR! LONG WALKS! COCKTAIL LUNCHES WITH THE GALS!"

"I DON'T LIKE ANY OF THOSE THINGS."

"SHUT UP. YOU ARE SUCH A **MIRANDA**."

"I THINK WHAT MAKES IT GOOD IS THAT IT DOESN'T LAST. THE BEST THINGS ARE RARE."

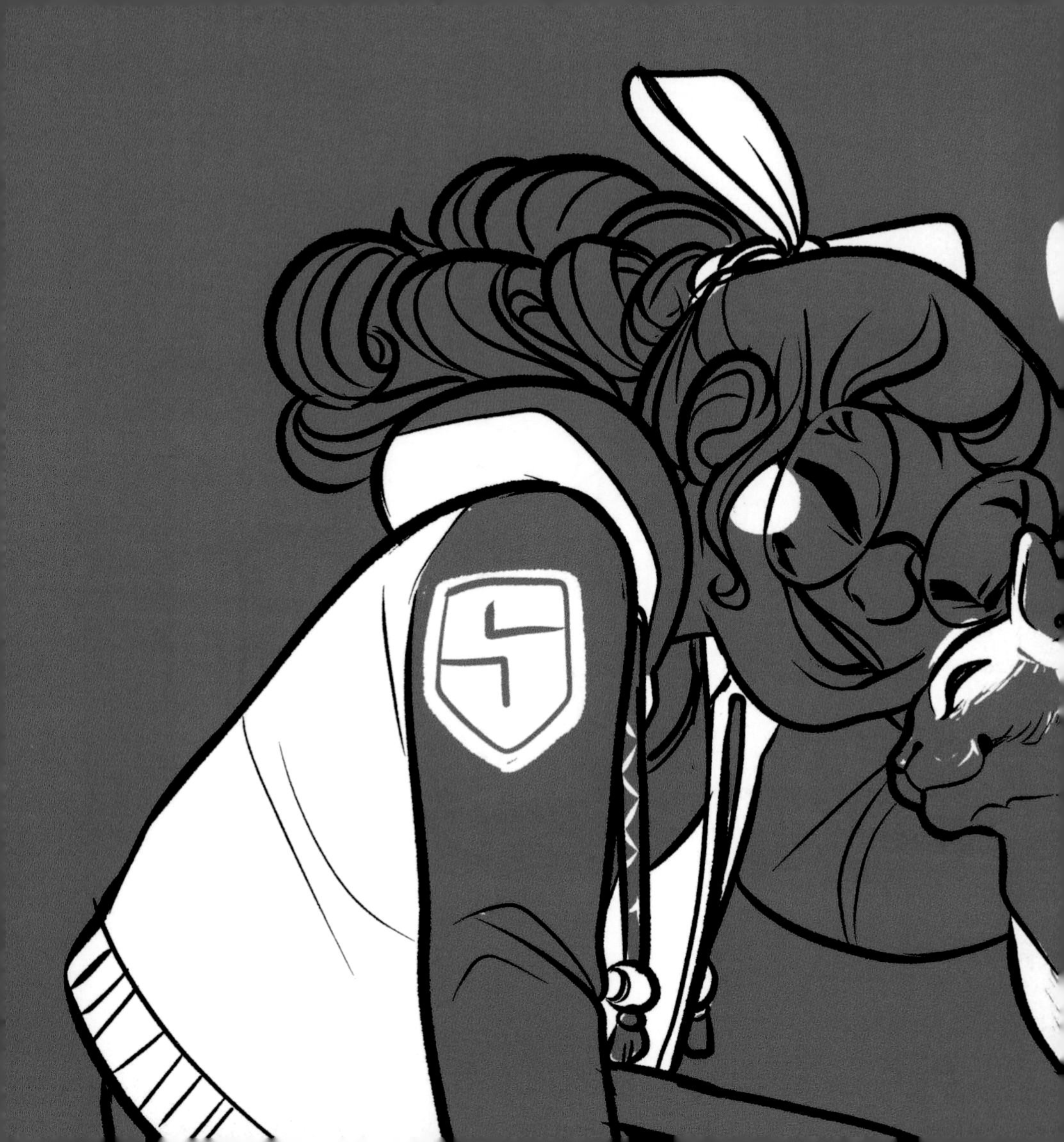

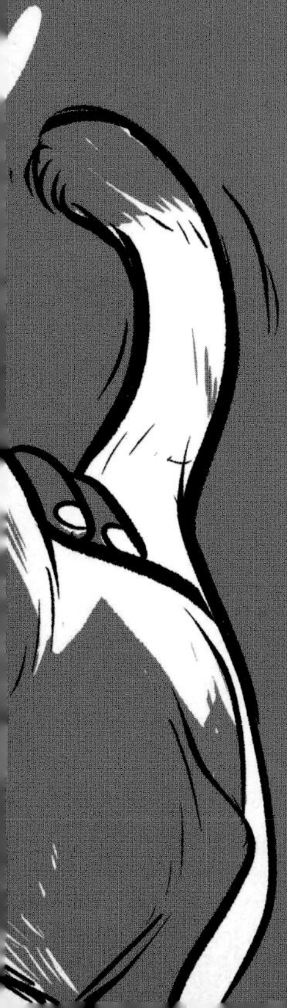

110% EVERYTHING ELSE

"THE PROBLEM WITH LIVING IN THE MOMENT IS THAT THERE'S SO LITTLE TIME TO THINK ABOUT WHAT YOU'RE GOING TO DO TOMORROW."

"IS THAT THE...MOON?
WHY IS IT ON FIRE?"

"THAT'S THE SUN.
YOU REMEMBER,
PHOEBUS' TORCH."

"I LIVE LIFE LIKE A BULLET TRAIN. YOU DON'T HAVE TIME TO PICK OUT THE DETAILS OUT OF THE WINDOW. I KNOW THERE'S SOMETHING OUT THERE, BUT IT'S...BLURRY."

"**NERDS**. I WENT IN A COMIC SHOP ONCE, DIDN'T LIKE IT. WALL TO WALL *DOCTOR WHO* DOLLS. ALL THE CHARACTERS. DOCCO. HAIRY MARY. BILL THE WASP. I WANTED A BOOK ABOUT THAT ORANGE CAT. LASAGNA CAT."

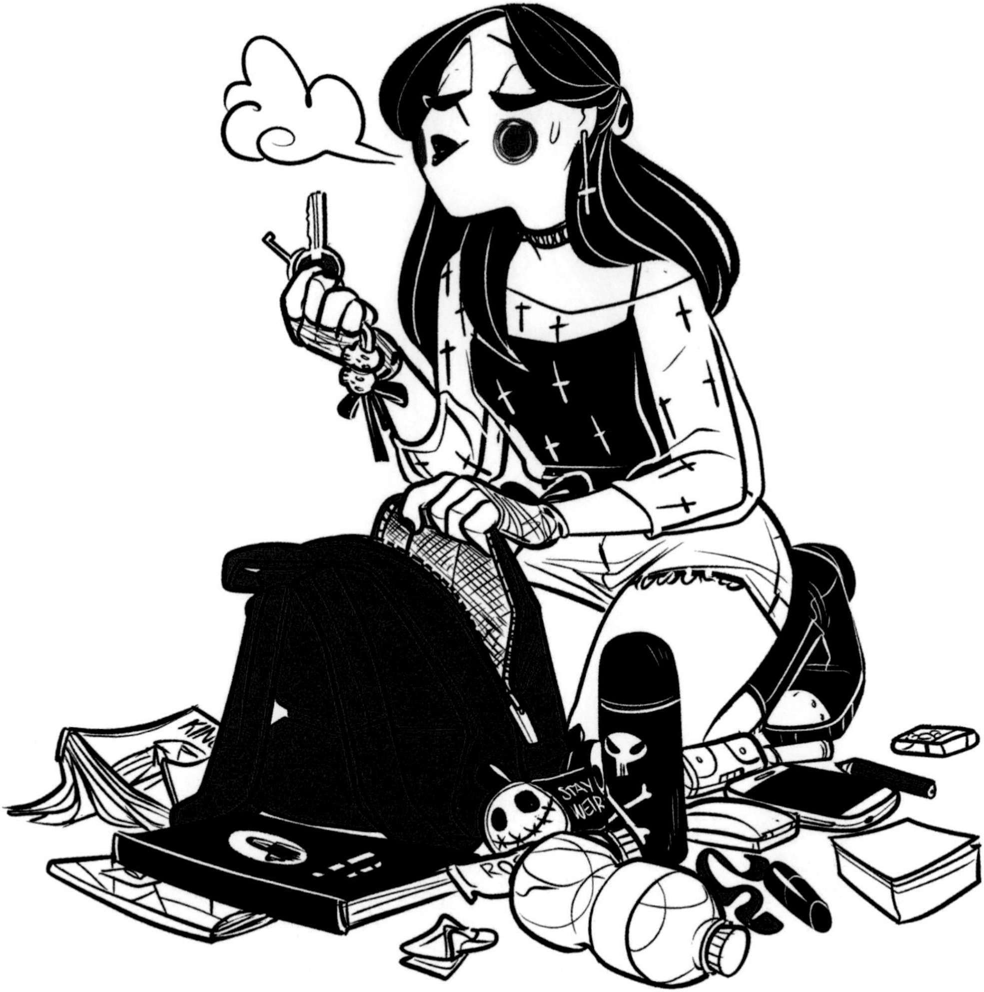
STAY WEIR

"WITH GREAT POWER COMES GREAT RESPONSIBILITY." TO QUOTE DR. BEN SPIDERMAN."

"I CAN'T TELL IF THAT'S PASSIVE, PASSIVE AGGRESSIVE, OR AGGRESSIVE."

"I JUST TRIED TO IMAGINE WHAT NELSON MANDELA WOULD DO!"

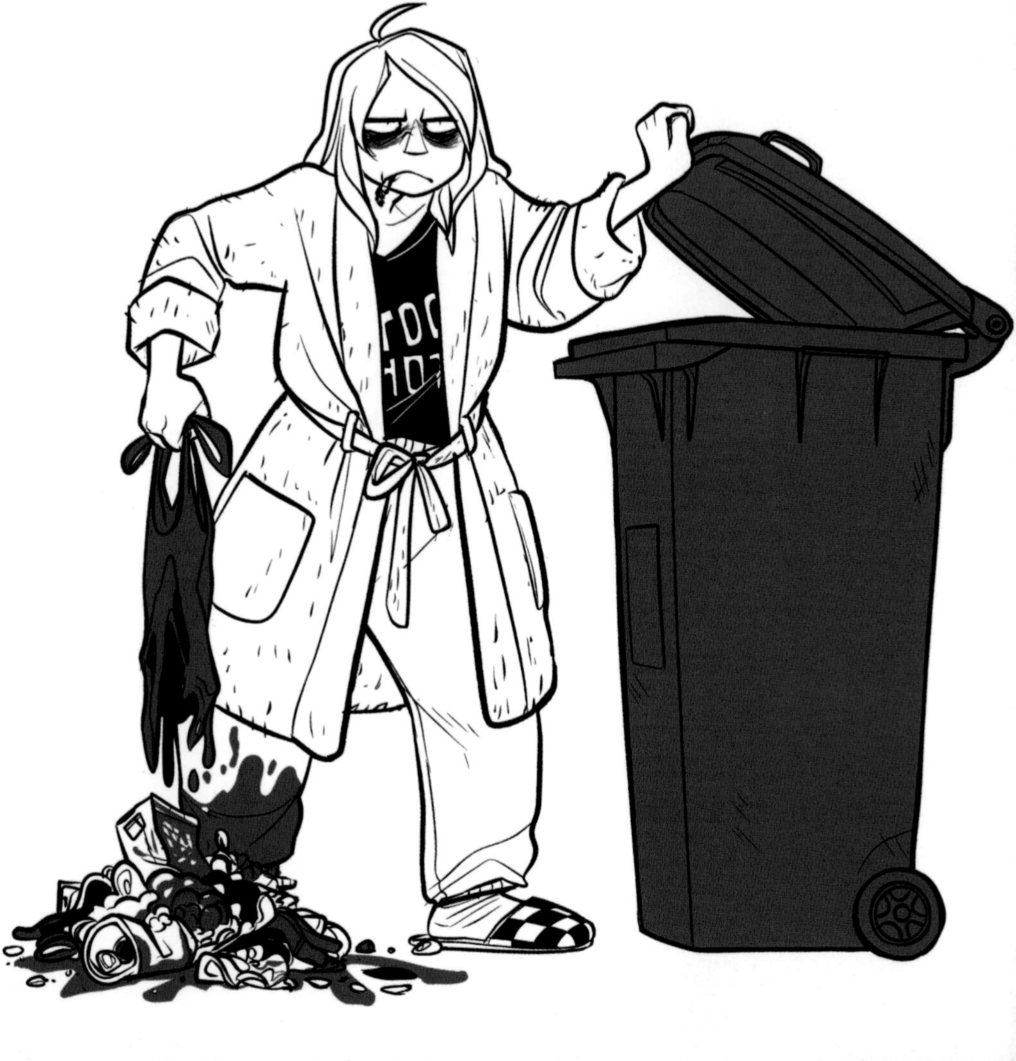

"YOU CAN'T MAKE AN OMELETTE WITHOUT PUNCHING A FEW IDIOTS."

"HISTORY HAS TAUGHT ME THAT PROBLEMS SHRINK THE FURTHER YOU RUN AWAY FROM THEM."

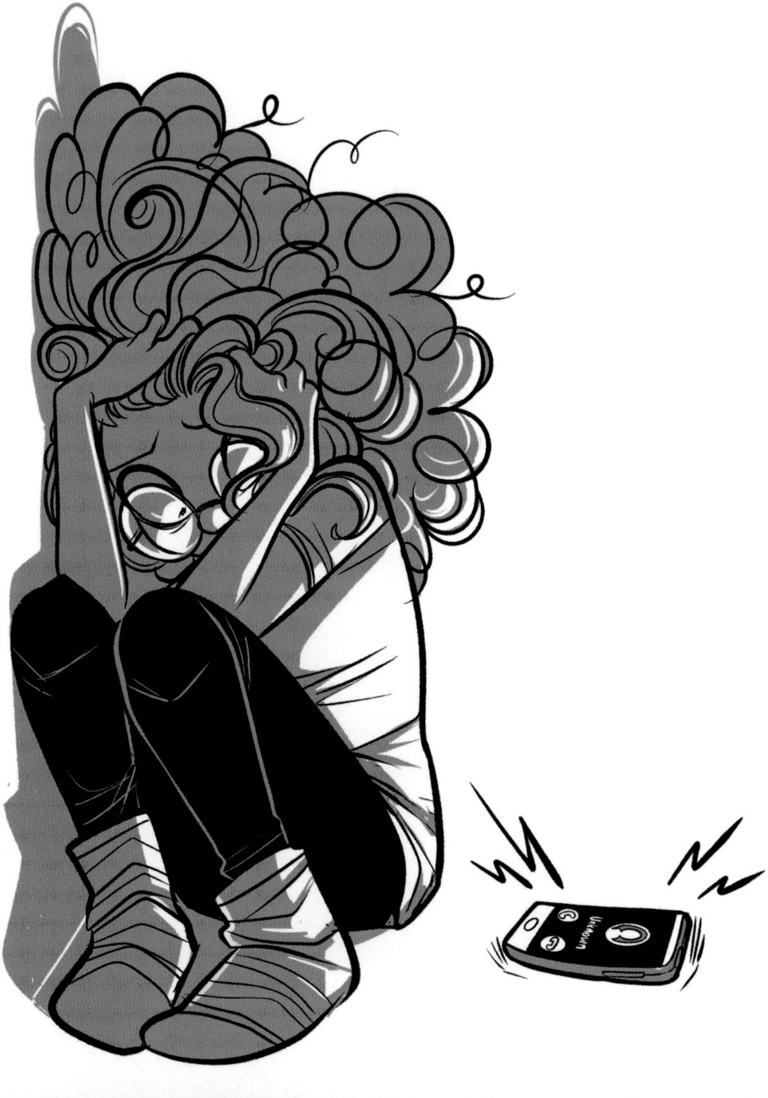
Unknown

"NGH, I USED TO HAVE SO MUCH SPACE IN MY HEAD, NOW IT'S JUST A WORRY WAREHOUSE!"

"ESTHER, HOW
WOULD YOU DESCRIBE
DAISY'S LOOK?"

"KIND YOUNG WOMAN CHIC"?

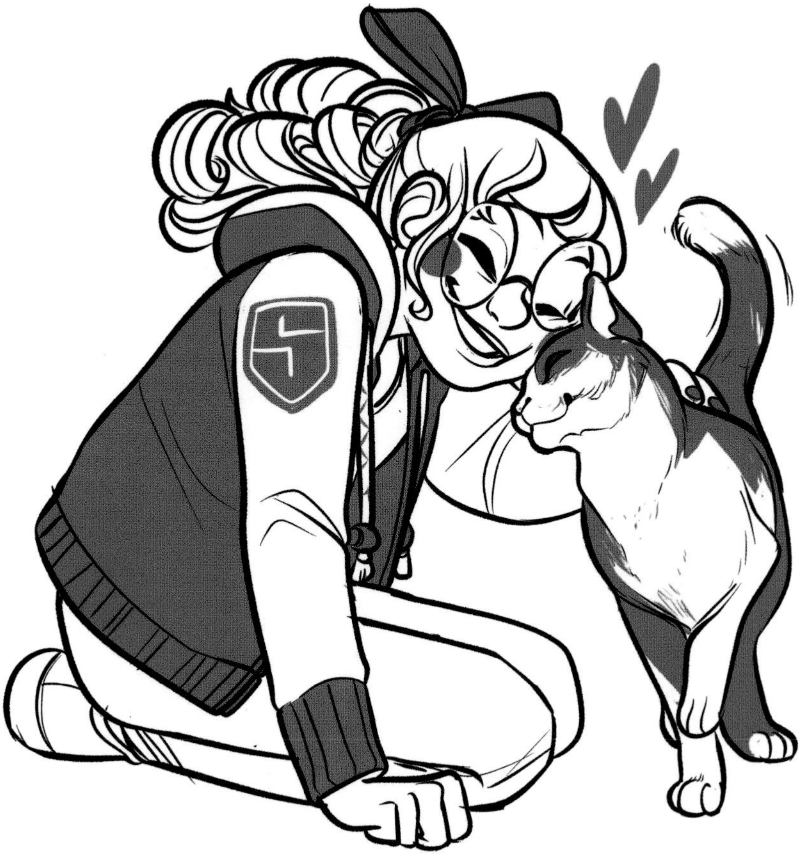

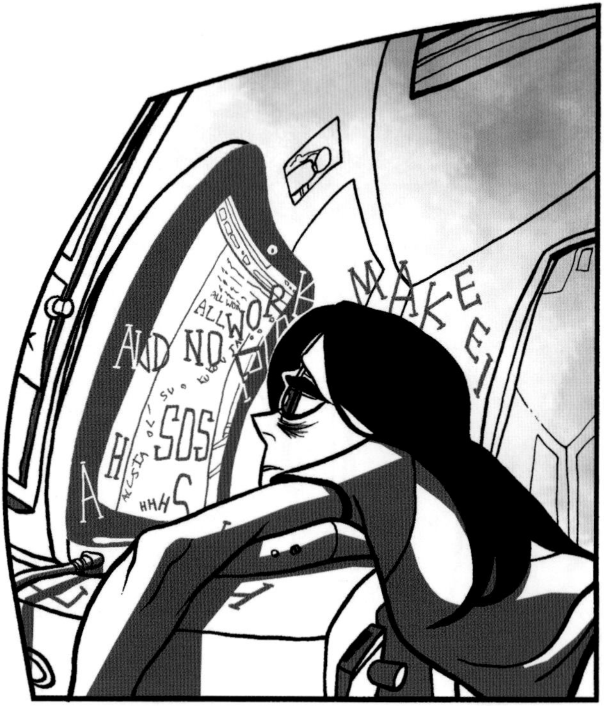
ALL WORK
AND NO
WORK
MAKE
SOS

"WHAT'S WRONG WITH ME?
THE INTERNET WILL KNOW!"

"THIS IS MY HATING BOOK.
IT'S A *GHOSTBUSTERS*-STYLE
CONTAINMENT UNIT
FOR MY RAGE."

"I CAN FEEL THE SADNESS
SPREADING INTO MY BONES.
MY...PEOPLE ARE VERY
PRONE TO THIS."

"GIVEN THE CHOICE BETWEEN GROUNDLESS OPTIMISM AND PROFOUND PESSIMISM... I HAVE DECIDED TO **DRINK**."

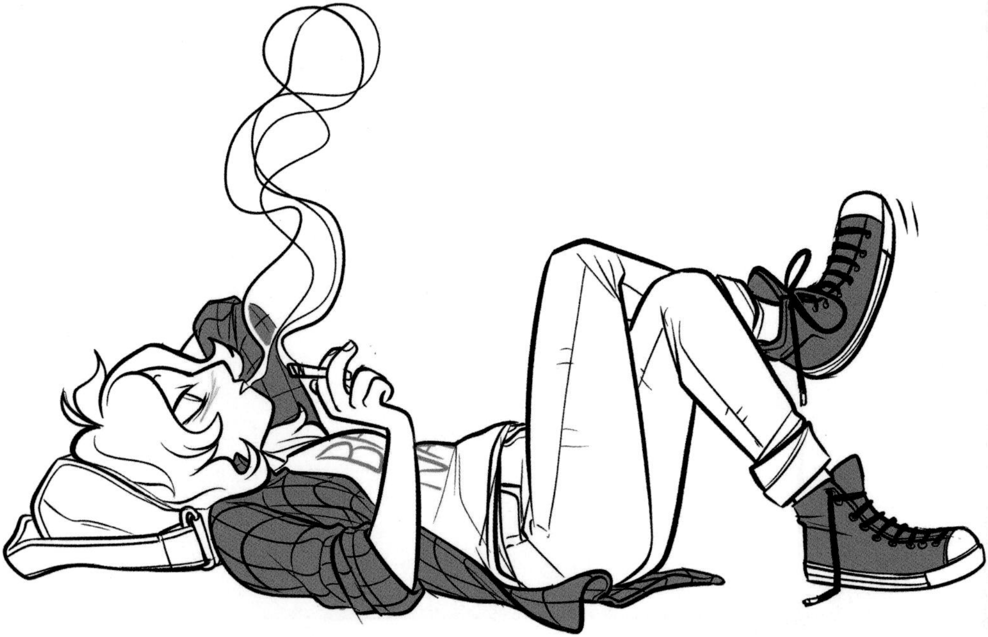

"CAN WE SHUT UP ABOUT THIS? TALK ABOUT ANYTHING ELSE. ARCHITECTURE! FEMMISM! WE'RE A WALKING ADVERT FOR THE BECHDEL TEST!"

"SHE NEEDS HER MISERY REST SO SHE CAN GET STRONG AND POWERFUL IN THE WORLD AGAIN. I SENSE... THAT SHE WILL LIVE."

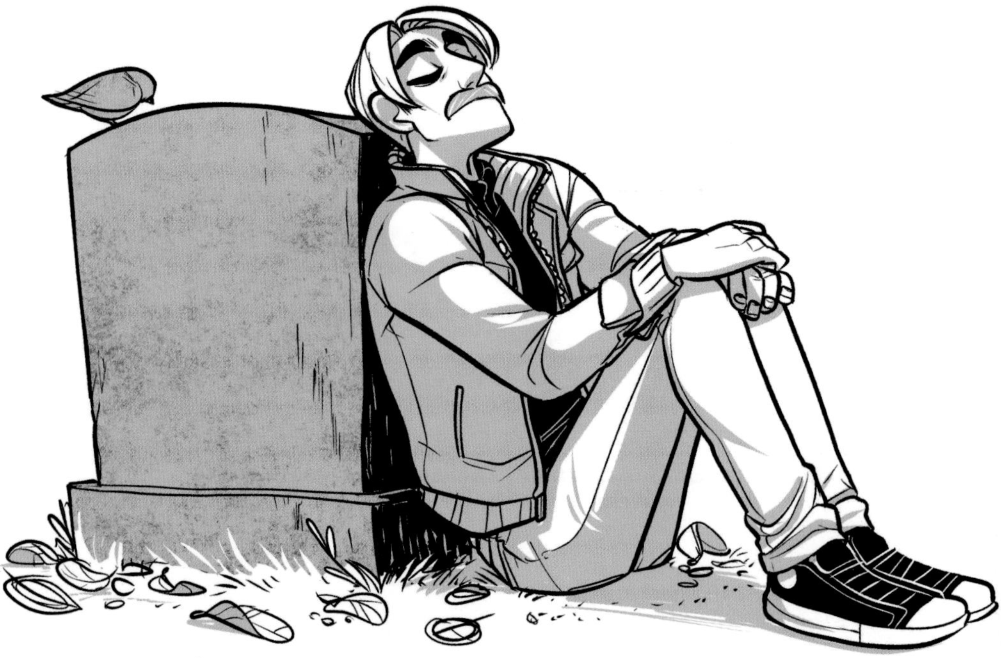

"I DON'T KNOW WHAT'S GOING ON IN MY HEAD FROM ONE MINUTE TO THE NEXT. BUT I THINK THAT LIFE HAS TO GET BIGGER TO MAKE DEATH SEEM SMALLER."

DISCOVER **ALL THE HITS**

Lumberjanes
Noelle Stevenson, Shannon Watters,
Grace Ellis, Brooklyn Allen, and Others
Volume 1: Beware the Kitten Holy
ISBN: 978-1-60886-687-8 | $14.99 US
Volume 2: Friendship to the Max
ISBN: 978-1-60886-737-0 | $14.99 US
Volume 3: A Terrible Plan
ISBN: 978-1-60886-803-2 | $14.99 US
Volume 4: Out of Time
ISBN: 978-1-60886-860-5 | $14.99 US
Volume 5: Band Together
ISBN: 978-1-60886-919-0 | $14.99 US

Giant Days
John Allison, Lissa Treiman, Max Sarin
Volume 1
ISBN: 978-1-60886-789-9 | $9.99 US
Volume 2
ISBN: 978-1-60886-804-9 | $14.99 US
Volume 3
ISBN: 978-1-60886-851-3 | $14.99 US

Jonesy
Sam Humphries, Caitlin Rose Boyle
Volume 1
ISBN: 978-1-60886-883-4 | $9.99 US
Volume 2
ISBN: 978-1-60886-999-2 | $14.99 US

Slam!
Pamela Ribon, Veronica Fish,
Brittany Peer
Volume 1
ISBN: 978-1-68415-004-5 | $14.99 US

Goldie Vance
Hope Larson, Brittney Williams
Volume 1
ISBN: 978-1-60886-898-8 | $9.99 US
Volume 2
ISBN: 978-1-60886-974-9 | $14.99 US

The Backstagers
James Tynion IV, Rian Sygh
Volume 1
ISBN: 978-1-60886-993-0 | $14.99 US

Tyson Hesse's Diesel: Ignition
Tyson Hesse
ISBN: 978-1-60886-907-7 | $14.99 US

Coady & The Creepies
Liz Prince, Amanda Kirk,
Hannah Fisher
ISBN: 978-1-68415-029-8 | $14.99 US

BOOM! BOX™

AVAILABLE AT YOUR LOCAL
COMICS SHOP AND BOOKSTORE
To find a comics shop in your area, visit www.comicshoplocator.com
WWW.**BOOM-STUDIOS**.COM

All works © their respective creators. BOOM! Box and the BOOM! Box logo are trademarks of Boom Entertainment, Inc. All rights reserved.